DATE LOA

OC4

9 MAY '65

25 Jan '44 W

5 Mar '4

P9-APO-378

Washington

Franklin

Rousseau

Saint-Simon

Jansen

Dante

Marx

MAZZINI

MAZZINI

THE LIVING THOUGHTS OF

MAZZINI,

Giuseppe.

PRESENTED BY

IGNAZIO SILONE

THE LIVING THOUGHTS LIBRARY

EDITED BY ALFRED O. MENDEL

1939

LONGMANS, GREEN AND CO.

NEW YORK · TORONTO

The Living Thoughts Library
is being published in Argentina (Spanish), Bulgaria, Canada, Czecho-slovakia, Denmark, Finland, France, Great Britain, Holland, Hungary, Norway, Poland, Rumania, Sweden, the United States of America, Yugoslavia

Translation of the Introductory Essay by Dr. Arthur Livingstone

The selections are from *Life and Writings of Joseph Mazzini,* published by Smith & Elder, 1864–1870

The woodcut portrait of Mazzini was made by Professor Hans A. Mueller

MAZZINI

COPYRIGHT · 1939 BY LONGMANS, GREEN AND CO., INC. ALL RIGHTS RESERVED, INCLUDING THE RIGHT TO REPRODUCE THIS BOOK, OR ANY PORTION THEREOF, IN ANY FORM

FIRST EDITION

PRINTED IN THE UNITED STATES OF AMERICA

320.8
M477s

DG
552
.8
m2918

Life travels upward in spirals. He who
takes pains to search the shadows of the
past below us, then, can better judge the
tiny arc up which he climbs, more surely
guess the dim curves of the future
above him.

273754

MAZZINI

"One morning in 1872," writes Jane Addams in
Forty Years at Hull-House (p. 21), "when I was
not yet twelve years old, I came into my father's
room to find him sitting beside the fire with a news-
paper in his hand, looking very solemn ; and upon
my eager inquiry what had happened, he told me
that Joseph Mazzini was dead. I had never even
heard Mazzini's name, and after being told about
him I was inclined to grow argumentative, asserting that my father did not know him, that he was
not an American, and that I could not understand
why we should be expected to feel badly about him.
It is impossible to recall the conversation with the
complete breakdown of my cheap arguments, but
in the end I obtained that which I have ever regarded as a valuable possession, a sense of the genuine relationship which may exist between men who
share large hopes and like desires, even though they
differ in nationality, language, and creed ; that those
things count for absolutely nothing between groups
of men who are trying to abolish slavery in America or to throw off Hapsburg oppression in Italy.
At any rate, I was heartily ashamed of my meagre
notion of patriotism, and I came out of the room

exhilarated with the consciousness that impersonal
and international relations are actual facts and not
mere phrases."

In the years between 1831 and 1849 Mazzini had
been the sincerest prophet and most devoted apostle of those "actual facts" in all Europe.   His private life had been closely identified with his political
and religious mission so that his name had become
a symbol and a battle slogan in most widely separated countries.   Carlyle had known him personally
in England.   The author of *Heroes and Hero Worship* did not agree with him in many respects ; but
when, as he tells us, he set out to find for his
masterpiece a countenance that could represent the
martyr under modern conditions of political and
social life, he could think of no face but Mazzini's.
Malvida von Meysenberg reports a somewhat similar judgment on Nietzsche's part : "Among all beautiful lives Nietzsche envied Mazzini's in a very
special way — that utter concentration upon a single idea that becomes as it were a flame in which
the whole individuality is consumed. Poets rid
themselves of their impulses to action by clothing
them in flesh in imaginative characters. They trans-
fer action and suffering outside themselves. With
Mazzini it was just the other way round. He ex-
pressed himself in his own life, and it became one
continuous realization in action of a most noble
personality. He was the tragic character in his own

drama, the one to accept the torture and the pain in the effort to achieve the ideal."

Mazzini had assumed the role of a national and humanitarian messiah in the light of a religious conception of life and history. The role turned, in fact, to tragedy after 1848. Then Italian national unity and independence began to take shape, not along the lines of the republicanism and the social revolution that he had preached, not as "sacred history of God and people," but under the leadership of Cavour, under the ægis of a dynasty, the House of Savoy, as a result of fortuitous diplomatic manoeuvres and compromises, and with the military assistance of self-seeking foreign powers. So it was with the social question. Mazzini had included social reform in his apostolate, timbering his platforms with utopian dreams after the manner of the early French socialists and particularly of the Saintsimonians. But actual events took a different course. The spirit of Marx and Bakunin came to prevail in the First International, which was founded during Mazzini's later years. He was not the man to follow success by changing principles — actually he was more interested in principles than in anything else. Little by little, therefore, his followers dropped away. His figure, which had once blazed so brilliantly before the public eye, grew dim in outline and faded into the background. His voice, which had once fiercely thundered in rebuke and prophecy, lost its force and its audience. During his last years people thought of him as definitely belonging to an age that had passed.

Later developments in European and Italian ways of thinking, along with a far-reaching reaction against "the stupid nineteenth century," tended to widen the breach between the rising generations and the complex of ideas and sentiments on which Mazzinianism had fed. A few people continued to call themselves Mazzinians in the twentieth century, but they merely repeated some of the political maxims of their master ; none of them professed his romantic faith. Perhaps the most vital elements in the inheritance that Mazzini left to his successors were his spirit of uncompromising opposition and his example of scrupulous and austere uprightness. But that attitude and outlook rarely have any great efficacy in politics. They made few converts. For one thing, the triumph of democratic institutions in Europe called for a different spirit from that which had prevailed in the day of conspiracies and secret societies. But then again, as regards Italy, the conflict of ideas and ideals lost much of its intensity. Socialists, republicans, and priests wooed the masses back and forth by organizing labor unions, co-operatives, and mutual aid societies, or else sought to satisfy purely local interests now in one way now in another. On all such matters Mazzini's teaching had nothing whatever to say.

II

And yet our remoteness from Mazzini's time and from the political problems that were then formulated, is, as we have recently come to see, only partial, and in many respects superficial, if not illusory. The present-day crisis in the structure of the capitalistic world is, to be sure, developing inside a basic framework of imperialisms ; but the situation has been quite unexpectedly complicated by belated upcroppings of problems that the nineteenth century left unsolved. One might state the specific problem of our age as the need of finding a political organization of the world that will correspond to our present high development of economic and social relations. Our failure, so far, to solve that problem has enabled the conservative elements in society to restore emphasis to many outmoded issues of the past century, such as problems of nationality or of socialistic projects of government control, and to mask a battle for their interests of class behind those issues. This strange and contradictory situation lends a most striking freshness to many forgotten pages of Mazzini, and the interest is only intensified by the fact that, in a number of European countries, today as a century ago, the spirit of freedom is forced to seek refuge in underground conspiracy. Of course, in reading or re-reading Mazzini in this light, one must, if one would avoid inevitable disappointment, be on one's guard against borrowing remedies for present evils. But under that petrified crust of philosophies, tastes, dreams, and errors peculiar to the era of romanticism, one is also certain to find more than one spark of a human aspiration that will endure as long as the human race endures.

III

Mazzini grew up during the years that followed the collapse of Napoleon's empire, years that were outwardly calm but were none the less pregnant with new conflicts. Reaction sat triumphant in all the countries of Europe. Conservatives everywhere were merrily applying themselves to restoring the old order and their old privileges, making free use of the police terror and intimidation that are characteristic of all reactions. However, the idea of freedom lived on — it lived on in the hearts of the veterans of the Napoleonic wars, for instance, and it continued to inspire the choicer elements in the intellectual classes, giving birth to a real florescence of philosophy and poetry. Police censorship was severe all over Europe ; but it was not able to prevent new ideas and new forms of art from crossing the frontiers of the nations and rearing against a "holy alliance" resting on bayonets, an "alliance of peoples" resting on a moral consciousness that was never merely passive, never merely contemplative. True morality is always a matter of action, and the morality of that day produced its men of action in goodly numbers, volunteers and conspirators who stood ready to meet reaction on the ground on which it had chosen to give battle — the ground of force.

Mazzini's cult of freedom may to an extent be ascribed to home influences. His father had been a member of the government under the Ligurian Republic (1797 to 1800) and had never forgotten those days. The mother was a devoted liberal, and so was Mazzini's Latin teacher, who had been a steadfast Jansenist all his life. However, even if a religious vocation may sometimes ripen gradually in a propitious environment, it often comes to the prophet in a flash, as a personal summons from on high. Mazzini has himself told of the circumstances under which he first felt the need of embracing the mission to which he was to devote his life. It was, says he, a Sunday of the month of April 1821. He was sixteen at the time. He was taking a walk with his mother and a friend of the family along a street in Genoa. A few days before, a mutiny of liberal army officers had broken out in the neighboring Piedmont. It had been instantly suppressed and the unlucky mutineers were flocking, penniless and with the police hot on their heels, into Genoa and other nearby coastal cities, hoping to find ways of embarking for Spain where, at the

moment, the liberal revolution was triumphant.
The refugees mingled in the festive Sunday crowds
trying to attract as little attention as possible. But
it was easy to pick them out by their provincial
traits, by the foreign cut of their clothes, and still
more by the fierce, intense expressions on their faces.
All of a sudden one of them approached the Mazzini party. He was a dark-complexioned, heavily
bearded individual, fiery-eyed, commanding, energetic. He made such an impression on young
Mazzini that forty years later the latter was still to
remember his name. He held out a taut-drawn
handkerchief before the three strollers and whis-
pered : "For the outlaws of Italy !" Gathering in
the coins that were proffered, he went on to other
groups.

That was Mazzini's moment of conversion, of
dedication to the struggle for his country's freedom.
His mind became obsessed, even at night in his
dreams, with his impression of those fugitives, men
who had been betrayed and defeated in their own
land, but who were by no means beaten, by no
means downhearted — they were merely trying to
reach another country where the fight for freedom
was still going on. People at the university, where
Mazzini was studying literature, began to notice
that he seemed suddenly older, that he was silent,
moody, absent-minded. He had taken to wearing
black suits and black ties, as though in mourning.

In his own heart in fact he had resolved to regard the woes of his country as a personal bereavement.

During those days he chanced upon the famous novel of Ugo Foscolo, *The Last Letters of Jacopo Ortis*, a work that breathed a melancholy tenderness after the manner of Goethe's *Werther*, but also an unhappy love of country. Mazzini read the book once and then a second time. Finally he set out to learn the text by heart, and the strange intensity with which he recited long passages led his mother to fear that he might be contemplating suicide. That, however, was just the tribute he was paying to a "world-weariness" which was the fad of the time. He was soon himself again. But he counted the book as among the main influences that had formed his character. Mazzini was a lad of delicate health and of a high-strung nervous temperament. Those physical traits were probably a congenial background for romanticism. But the great fact is that at that time all young men were romantics, in style of dress, in tastes, in morals, in conduct. Grandiloquent phrases, appeals to the sublime, fatal passions, oaths of eternal fidelity, moonlight meditations in cemeteries, eyes looking intensely out upon the eternal verities from the pallor of wan faces — all that was the order of the day. Romantic attitudes and impulses are conspicuous in Mazzini's biography down to his very last years; though perhaps one should not overstress their importance, since they are just the outer covering, so to say, of a deeper literary, ethical and religious romanticism, which was Mazzini's great glory and his great fight, the mission that gave shape to his life as a whole.

IV

Mazzini wrote his first article when he was twenty-one. It dealt with Dante, whom Mazzini revered not only as a poet but as "the father of his country." "In 1827," he later wrote, "the war between classicists and romanticists was at its height, the former defending a literary despotism that went back some two thousand years, the latter struggling to escape that despotism in favor of their own inspiration. We youngsters were all romanticists." Those were the days of Manzoni's *The Betrothed*, a novel that was to remain the most charming and enduring expression of Italian romanticism. Very soon, however, the romantic movement in Italy took on a predominantly political and social coloring and is hardly to be distinguished from the movement for Italian unity and independence. In one way or another Italian romantic literature, which is of second-rate quality on the whole, is a patriotic literature. The case of Mazzini would be typical of most Italian intellectuals of that period. His decision to abandon letters in favor of political agitation was deliberate, carefully considered — he

was later to call it the great sacrifice of his life.
That he had real talent for literary criticism, and
perhaps for imaginative writing, is amply proved
by the articles he published as a boy in the *Indicatore* of Genoa, and after the suppression of that
paper by the police, in the *Indicatore* of Leghorn.
In after years, in England, he was to have no difficulty in earning a living with his pen. He contributed to all the leading English magazines. However,
the many projects with which his mind flirted in
his youth — ideas for plays, historical novels, other
literary fancies — came to nothing; and he tried to
justify his failure to execute them with the theory
that in countries that are subject to foreign rule
there can be prophets, perhaps, but never artists.
"Art," he wrote, "is not the mere caprice of this or
that individual. It is either a solemn page of history or else a prophecy." And he went on to
argue that if art chances to fulfil that twin mission,
as he thought it had everywhere in Dante and here
and there in Byron, it becomes supreme art.

As for Italy, he thought art could be nothing, if
not prophetic. For three centuries Italians had
had no spontaneous life of their own. They had
been just stupefied slaves, eating out of the hand of
the foreigner. Art could come to life only by
shouting its curse upon those three centuries and
striking the keynote for the song of the future. In
order to do that it had to reach down into the

latent, unconscious, slumbering life of the people, lay its hand upon the frozen heart of the nation, catch the infrequent and barely perceptible palpitations there, and come forth with noble ideals and sound guiding principles for the better minds. Individual inspiration ought to spring from the collective life of the nation, much as flowers, the poems of the earth, beautiful in their varying and strictly individual colorings, spring from the national soil. But it was hard to speak of a collective life in the case of Italy. There there was no centre of thought and feeling, no unity, no regular and orderly expression. There might be isolated, volcanic outbursts of art now here now there, but nothing continuous or progressive — and Mazzini mentioned the luxuriant jungles of the New World where the trees twined branch with branch to create the gigantic unity of the tropical forest. A people without a country, without freedom, might have forerunners of art, prophets of art, hardly artists. It was better, therefore, for intellectuals to concentrate on the problem : "Are we to have a country ?" If they succeeded in creating one, then art would blossom after their time and provide, as it was, the flowers for their tombs.

Today one might consider this theory naive, if not frankly false ; but in its very vagueness it succeeded in imparting a striking message. It implied that it was time for Italians to have done with a

literature which was a mere ornament or entertain-
ment for court life, which merely flattered the instincts of an idle, skeptical, fatuous ruling class, and
to go looking for an active militant literature that
would come close to the people and perform a real
social and educational function.   However, in Mazzini's time, to speak of an Italian people was to
speak of a mass of illiterates brutalized by poverty
and superstition. To make free citizens of virtual
slaves something more than plays with a purpose
and novels with a thesis was called for. Even in
environments that are far more enlightened than
Mazzini's was, any educated man whose love of
beauty goes hand in hand with love of truth and a
decent interest in being useful to his fellowmen has
to make his choice between the cult of letters and
the active life. Does it mean anything just to
write ? For whom is one to write ? Shall one
make books — or why not bombs ? There are
those who die for freedom, and there are those who
write about those who die for freedom. Sometimes, to be sure, one notes a book that is as important in its effects as a decisive battle.

v

"Mazzini," says Salvemini, "took from the philosophies, political theories and histories that were
in fashion about him, such elements as seemed to

fit in with his temperament, and he organized them into a structure that was coherent enough to meet the practical requirements of his career." Mazzini's mother was a Jansenist and, as we saw, had Jansenists about her, so creating an environment that was severe, austere, devoutly religious. A sensitive child, Mazzini naturally responded to these pressures and grew up with concepts of life that were definitely moralistic on a background of Christian piety. As time went on he filled out his moral world with a number of philosophical or mythological concepts as to Divine Providence or Humanity that he had more or less thoroughly assimilated from such writers as Joseph de Maistre and other ideologues of the Restoration. That was an era of religious revival, so called, and almost all writers, whether liberal or reactionary, felt its influence.

The source of the revival is easily recognizable. It lay in the political disaster that had come upon the ideas and institutions issuing from the French Revolution. The failure of a revolution regularly discourages and humiliates mankind. People lose confidence in themselves. They are convinced anew of their weakness, their unworthiness, their worthlessness. And all that turns to the advantage of the priest, who finds his lambs returning to the fold, repentant, bewildered, and much the worse for wear. The fall of Napoleon stood there to prove that human history has its laws and that such

laws cannot be overborne even by a man of talent.
If at times the laws of history seem to suffer lapses
or periods of suspension, that is just a way Divine
Patience has of admonishing men, just a way it has
devised — anticipating, in this respect, many doctrines of modern education — for making men understand how badly off they would be, what dis-
asters would come upon them, if they were left to
govern themselves. In the religious revivals that
follow wars and revolutions two elements are always present : the homesickness of the swineherd
prodigal for his father's house ; and then a Machiavellian instinct in the ruling classes, who are other-
wise skeptics and unbelievers but nevertheless
understand that the fear of God is the best of all
policemen when it comes to keeping the poorer
classes resigned to their lot in life.

Mazzini had an eminently instrumental conception of the Divinity, but in a sense counter to that
of the reactionaries. One of Mazzini's keenest crit-
ics, Francesco de Sanctis, once pointed to a letter
that Mazzini wrote to Sismondi as proof that the
God to whom prayers were addressed in the propaganda of the Mazzinians was a political entity.
That, perhaps, would be going too far. No mere
private letter would be sufficient to cast doubt upon
the sincerity of a religious faith to which Mazzini's
life bears witness throughout its whole course.
Mazzini was a moralist before being a statesman

and he was always more of a moralist than a states-man. Before Mazzini became general manager and superintendent of the various independence movements in Europe, his God was an imperious postulate of Mazzini's conscience — He was infinite Morality, infinite Love, infinite Justice, Guide to history, and Teacher of men along the pathways to perfection. At times the Deity invoked by Mazzini is conspicuously pantheistic, interchangeable with Law, natural and human, and to be worshipped in the harmony of the cosmos. At other times, Mazzini was aware that pantheism presupposed oneness in the universe, therefore oneness of subject and object, of Creator and created, and, therefore also, absence of freedom. Whenever this implication came to weigh on his mind, his moral sense would revolt and he would turn to a personal, transcendent God, God the Father of all, God the Judge of all. Since Mazzini was not primarily a philosopher, these inconsistencies, this fluttering back and forth between pantheism and theism, never caused him any great mental strain; much less did they dampen or cool his ardent religious faith. As Crespi, one of his most loyal interpreters, puts it, Mazzini drew on both those philosophies for nutriment for his intense spiritual life, using the personal God to whet and sustain his sense of duty, and the cosmic God to fortify his often quailing heart with certainty in ultimate victory. In Mazzini's view there could be no human brotherhood apart from religion. Not only did morality "need a heaven and a dogma to support it"; no real society could exist without common beliefs, common aspirations. Truth cannot be discovered by the intellect. It is immanent in the heart of men, where it has been placed by God. Can we know that God exists? "God exists," answers Mazzini. "We do not need to prove it to you. We are not going to try to prove it to you. To try to do such a thing seems to us blasphemous, just as to deny the existence of God seems to us madness. A person who could stand before a starry night, beside the grave of a dear one, or in the presence of suffering for a noble cause, and then deny God would be a very unfortunate and a very wicked person."

Mazzini's strong sense of fairness kept him from falling in with one of the basic doctrines of reactionary religion — the question of expiation. According to Joseph de Maistre, human suffering is a just penalty which men cannot escape and should not try to escape. Any real progress is impossible because of the sinfulness of human nature. Such an unappealable condemnation of mankind seemed monstrous to Mazzini, something utterly unworthy of God, "who could not be aught else" than Infinite Love for all created beings. Mazzini regarded life on earth as a continuous process of growth toward spiritual perfection, a process of "angelification," as he called it. Humanity could not help advancing step by step along a pathway toward ultimate happiness and goodness which Providence had pre-surveyed. "The successive generations of human beings, born of Him and brethren of each other in capacities and impulses, pass to each other, now the more now the less radiant according to times and abilities, the Torch of Life that has issued from Him and is ever kindled anew and fed by His spirit."

Prerequisite to this type of progress would be a recognition in public life of the superiority of spiritual over all other values ; and that premise led inexorably to a very embarrassing consequence where Mazzini found himself on common ground with Joseph de Maistre, namely, that civil power should be subordinated to religious authority. De Maistre had argued that peace, morality, and the stability of institutions could be achieved only if they were withdrawn from lay control and made subject to religious investiture. That was far from being a new theory, but the course of events between 1789 and 1831 seemed to supply striking confirmation of it ; and De Maistre went on to formulate his doctrine of the Pope as the absolute sovereign over all earthly sovereigns. Mazzini, too, admitted that the authority of one man over another could be justifiable only as delegated by God. "Nothing belongs to Cæsar save in accordance with divine law," he wrote. "Cæsar, in other words, temporal power, what we call government, is nothing but the mandatory of God, the executive, so far as times and abilities permit, of God's plans." Cavour, who was a consistent liberal, was one day to proclaim the principle of "a free church in a free state." Mazzini called that doctrine "deadly," "disgraceful," "base," "acceptable only to men devoid of any spark of moral conviction."

However, the religious authority to which he would have subordinated the governments of the peoples was not the Catholic papacy, nor any of the other churches existing — they were all too imperfect as compared with the high and absolute ideal he cherished in his heart. He often writes of his great reverence for Jesus, but he never called himself a Christian and he refused to admit the divinity of Christ. To an intimate he once wrote : "I profess a faith which I consider purer and loftier than Christianity, but its time is not yet come." Bolton King, Mazzini's best biographer, writes that of Christianity "he retained its belief in the omnipotence of the spiritual ; its faith in God and in His providential working ; its supreme veneration for the character and moral teaching of Jesus ; its insistence on moral perfection and not material interest as the end of life ; its call to love and sacrifice of self ; its belief in immortality ; its aspiration to the Church Universal." As for the papacy, Mazzini judged it as "condemned beyond recall or appeal." Christianity, he thought, had fulfilled its "historic mission," its "revolutionary energies were therefore exhausted." "Science," he wrote in 1870, in an open letter to the Vatican Council, "is progressing, forgetful of your teachings, indifferent to your anathemas and your councils, tearing up at each new discovery one more page of the book you declare infallible. Art now gropes blindly in void, now retreats upon pagan ideals, now, tottering, starts in pursuit of some fanciful religious inspiration, or finally, in despair of finding any God, tries to worship itself; but wherever it goes, whatever it does, it remains outside Christianity and makes no response to the ideas that centuries ago inspired your architects and your painters. Governments repudiate you in the exercise of their power. The men among you who are most intelligent or eloquent are deserting you one by one. Not one of the great advances made in our day have been promoted by your utterance or dedicated to your word. Like sphinxes in a boundless desert you sit inertly gazing upon the ghosts of ages that have passed."

Mazzini got from Saint Simon the utopian idea of a theocracy emanating directly from the people. "The Holy Church of the Future, the Church of the Free and Equal, will give its blessing to every forward step that is taken by the Spirit of Truth.

It will be one with the life of Humanity. It will
have no popes and no laity, but just believers. All
men will be priests with differing functions. And
there will be a new heaven and a new earth." This
was not the first time, surely, that the coming of
the kingdom of God upon this earth had been
preached in just such language. Within Catholicism itself, from the day of Saint Joachim on, and
in spite of the dictatorship of a worldly, jesuitical
and unity-loving hierarchy, that dream had never
been lost sight of, especially in some of the monastic
orders. But the rebirth foretold by Mazzini dif-
fered in essential respects from the earlier ones.
His vision implied a far-reaching condemnation of
the whole social order of his day, a condemnation
both of churches and of governments. Upon his
converts he enjoined not contemplation and prayer
in solitude, but struggle, unending struggle, struggle without quarter, even at the expense of the
greatest personal sacrifices. For the advent of his
new Jerusalem he looked not to a miraculous intervention of God but to riots, insurrections, revolutions by the peoples conceived as the motive forces
of the divine will. From the historical standpoint,
Mazzini's utopia was a world in which there would
be nothing but free peoples. To them he trans-
ferred the religious legitimacy and authority which
he withdrew from the papacy and from the dynasties that ruled in his time.

VI

"In Europe, today," wrote Mazzini, "the word revolution is synonymous with the word nationality. It implies a redrawing of the map of Europe ; a cancellation of all treaties based on conquest, compromise, and the wills of reigning houses ; a reorganization to be made in line with the temperaments and capabilities of the peoples and with their free consent ; a removal of the causes of selfish hostility among the peoples ; a balancing of power among them, and therefore the possibility of brotherhood. The sovereignty of that goal must replace the sovereignty of force, caprice and chance."

In line with that attitude Mazzini became the champion of all oppressed nationalities. The causes of Croatia, Bohemia, Hungary, Poland, he embraced and defended along with the cause of Italy. One must observe, however, and in most emphatic terms, that the various schools of modern nationalism based on biological or racial myths have no reason to regard Mazzini as one of their forefathers. A criterion of race can serve, at the most, for classifying horses. Neither geography nor language nor religion is alone adequate for constituting nationality. One cannot deny that the Swiss people constitutes a nation, yet it speaks four languages, is part Protestant, part Catholic, and at a number of points in Switzerland cannot be said to have clearly definable frontiers. Nationality is an historical phenomenon resulting from a given evolution of human civilization within certain limits of time and space. For Mazzini the original germ of nationality lay in the consciousness of a common calling, or mission. "Nationality is the share that God has assigned to the given people in the progress of humanity. It is the mission which each people must fulfill, the task it must do, on earth, that the divine idea may attain its full expression; it is the work which gives a people a right to citizenship in the world. It is the sign of that people's personality and of the rank it occupies among other peoples, its brothers." The more tenaciously a people cherished the consciousness of its mission, even under the rule of foreign peoples, the nobler would be the message that God would entrust to it for the betterment of all. "In the fullness of time the people that has most suffered and has kept its faith the purest, will be blessed by God with the will and the courage to conquer and die for all. Such is the people that innovates. It rises and fights. It may triumph or it may perish, but either from its ashes or from its altar of victory the Word which is the Word of the era goes forth — and the world is saved."

Mazzini imagined his prophet people calling a world conference, a real "Council of Humanity," to be attended by "those who are the best in wisdom and virtue among those who believe in eternal things, in the mission of God's creature upon earth, in the worship of progressive Truth. And these will assemble reverently to feel the soul pulse of collective humanity and to ask of those peoples who feel a stirring within them but are uncertain of themselves and of the future : 'How much of the old faith has died in your hearts? How much of the faith of the future has begun to live in you?' "

A certain kinship of spirit and language may be noticed between the messianic proclamations of Mazzini and the philosophy of Polish nationalism as preached about that very time by Mickiewicz and Cieszkowski, a definitely messianic doctrine which, in view of peculiar circumstances in Poland, continues to count followers there even today. Never before that time had sentiments of nationality been so lavishly exalted. But those patriots, it should be noted, did not think of a nation as asserting itself at the expense of humanity. In view of the fact that each nation had been created by God's will, each nation was subordinate to a divine plan of universal utility. To violate the rights of another people was to do harm to society as a whole and therefore to oneself. The nationalisms so popular in our time are exclusivist, chauvinist, xenophobic, antisemitic, imperialist — in a word, reactionary. The nationalism of Mazzini was tolerant, conciliatory, humanitarian, cosmopolitan, progressive. There is little in common between the two systems. Modern nationalism is showing itself to be the real enemy of nations.

Nor should one, following superficial points of contact, confuse the "primacy" which in the nineteenth century Mazzini and Gioberti claimed for Italy, Guizot for France, Fichte for Germany, and Hirzel for Switzerland, with the aspirations to world dominion of the imperialistic powers of our time. Primacy was then conceived as the right and the duty of a nation to lead other peoples on the road to human perfection. In fact the Germans grounded the superiority of their nation as a civilizing force on the mixed character of the German population. "The law of duty," said Mazzini, "once it has been acknowledged and embraced will supplant the impulse to usurp the rights of others which has so far prevailed in the relations of people with people. The controlling principle in public policy will be not the weakening of others, but the betterment of all through the efforts of all, in other words, the progress of each to the advantage of all. Political world unity is inconceivable as the military supremacy of one power over all the others, for no people can in the long run be resigned to oppression and exploitation by others. Co-operation and peace will reign on earth only through the association of the peoples and on the condition that they shall be free and equal. Humanity will really attain organized existence only when all peoples have achieved the free exercise of their sovereignty and become associates in a republican federation."

Mazzini stated and developed that theory on many occasions. If one might have a right to doubt that there is any great probability of seeing his dream realized in our time, one would not have a right to cite in evidence the failure of the so-called League of Nations. That League, one should not forget, was a League of mere governments — and, bless us! what governments! Before they have been swept away, there can be no serious talk of a society of nations.

VII

In common with all the thinkers of his day Mazzini conceived of history as evolving by epochs and stages according to a pre-established design. He justified his life work by an appeal to God, whereas others of his contemporaries professed to follow the dictates of science, of history, of political economy. Looking back upon all that cerebration objectively, and from the vantage point of today, we can see that those systems of thought were all differing but equivalent devices for strengthening one's own hand and inspiring confidence and courage in one's followers. The passing years have shown that the famed "laws" of history and positive sci-

ence are as mythological as the commandments of
the faiths and that they are just as much products of
passion, imagination, aspiration as was the Divine
Providence of Mazzini.

"Heaven helps the man who helps himself" was
the motto of a group of young liberals headed by
Guizot. From Guizot, as well as from Cousin and
Jouffroy and the men who foregathered at the
"Globe," Mazzini borrowed many phrases and slogans that had a liberal cast. He broke with them
when they rallied to the July Monarchy, denounc-
ing them as opportunists whom the facts had left
stranded. From Lamennais he learned the weak-
nesses of the rationalists and materialists of the
eighteenth century, but in the end he quarrelled
with that leader too, refusing to follow him in what
he called the "fatuous and pernicious illusion" that
Roman Catholicism could be harmonized with freedom. Mazzini readily succumbed to the lure of
Rousseau's belief in the natural goodness of mankind ; and he foresaw that as the masses were
brought into active participation in social life they
would contribute fresh spiritual energies which
would be of the greatest benefit to the moral at-
mosphere of the future. At the same time he was
always emphasizing cultural values which, unlike
the lilies of the field or the coal in the mines underground, are not spontaneous products of nature.
From Saint Simon and from that thinker's disciples,

Mazzini borrowed his aversion to struggles of classes and to the economic anarchy of capitalism, upholding the principle that opposing interests should come to terms and try to work together in the interests of social unity and peace for all humanity. Yet never once did Mazzini cease preaching freedom — and what can freedom amount to, if struggles and reasons for struggling are done away with ? Meantime he explicitly condemned the exploitation of labor and the parasitism of the wealthy.

"In spite of all that," says Croce, "in spite of the fact that Mazzini was not a coherent thinker and not a statesman, he rose to a position of intellectual, moral, and even political leadership in Europe. Patriots and revolutionists in all countries looked to him as to their master, while the absolutist and conservative governments made daily war upon him with their spies and their stool pigeons." The ideas that he gathered in from a hodgepodge of varied readings were contradictory and in themselves harmless, but they became high explosives in the pamphlets and propaganda sheets that he printed for the groups in Italy. He was not a teacher of sound thinking, he was a teacher of noble living — and that is the value that he still has today. In his day there were, as there are in ours, parlor revolutionaries and melodrama conspirators who looked at the papers every morning to see whether some great change had not taken place in the world.   In his day as in ours there were the politicians who ever play safe, the manœuvrers, the strategists, the "well-informed," who think instinctively in terms of diplomatic intrigues and calculation. Against all such Mazzini cried aloud that a people suffering under tyranny, whether domestic or foreign, could never win real freedom unless an elite of high-minded individuals was available to educate, inspire, and arouse the masses and lead them to open combat and self-sacrifice. Liberty is never received as a gift. It has to be fought for.

The failures of the insurrections of 1820, 1821, and 1830 in Piedmont, Naples, Spain, and Romagna convinced Mazzini that a radical change was necessary in ways of conceiving the revolutionary movement and in manners of leading it. The Carboneria had been a secret society. Its leaders had continued eighteenth-century ways of thinking while its rank and file was made up of timid businessmen who looked askance at any movement in which the masses participated. The agitation of the Carbonari therefore ended in a sort of ritualism of Masonic type, as complicated as it was fatuous, along with intrigues through secret "contacts" within this or that "friendly" government. In 1832 Mazzini founded his "Young Italy," a society that was necessarily more or less secret, to be sure, in order to escape destruction by Metternich's police but which basically was a propaganda movement, asserting and spreading ideas and appealing to the working classes in the towns.

Switzerland, France, and England were in those days crowded with refugees from the reactionary countries. Such people, as a rule, looked to the French government to bring about the European revolution. That was a comfortable illusion, and all the more harmful in that a very considerable body of fact was there to uphold it. The merciless repression that had been visited upon the liberal disturbances of the 1820's and early 1830's had broken up and dispersed local revolutionary organizations in the various countries, and such contacts as the exiles could arrange with comrades at home gave no promise of any effective or immediate resumption of the struggle.

Meantime not a few French publicists were devoting their rhetoric to advertising the liberating "mission" of France. According to Guizot, France was "the centre and home of European civilization." According to Bouchez, France "alone was able to understand a disinterested foreign policy and follow one." The "Grand Firmament" of Paris, of which Lafayette was president, had become a propaganda agency for asserting the solidarity of France with all oppressed peoples. Committees of sympathizers with the causes of free Italy and free Poland sprang up on every hand, and there were statesmen and even government ministers who as-

sured the exiles over and over again that if Louis
Philippe ever got to the throne he would, at the
proper moment, demonstrate in action his loyalty
to the civilizing tradition of France. The French
government formally announced that it would op-
pose any foreign intervention in countries where
a people had risen in behalf of its independence.

So, shortly after the July Revolution (1830), the
liberals in Belgium, Italy, Poland, rose as by common accord and in the firm persuasion that help
from France would be forthcoming. What a disappointment, therefore, when the armies of Austria
and Russia calmly invaded Poland and Italy and
brutally suppressed the independence movements,
without a protest, let alone armed opposition, from
France ! Indeed a French minister, in explaining
the government's policy, declared that "French
blood belonged to France," and cynically noted
that "order reigned in Warsaw." All the same,
for all of its sudden scruples about interference in
the "internal" affairs of other countries, the French
government in accord with England did intervene
in Belgium where French interests happened to be
involved, and helped that country to free itself of
the yoke of Holland in order to become a satellite
of France. Bitterness and disgust over the French
"betrayal" demoralized and paralysed many Italian
and Polish liberals for a long time to come ; but unfortunately, not to the point where the dismal delu-

sion of foreign help has been completely uprooted
from their minds.

It is worth while to remember the alibis, the ac-
cusations and counter-accusations which have kept
alive in the democratic press the polemic on the
bloody and grotesque farce of non-intervention.
Readers scanning the opinions of the official organs
in the recent case in Spain can find there the same
artifices, the same falsehoods, and the same shame-
lessness of those times. One can even say that they
were perpetrated by the same kind of men. The
platitudes, the gestures, the facial expressions, the
tones of voice, the dramatic method of playing of-
fended innocence and despised truth by the statesmen of today resemble in every detail the very same
methods of other days. From the good king Louis
Philippe to Comrade Léon Blum, political morals
have not changed much. Unchanged also is the
inexhaustible capacity of the exiles for illusion. If
St. Thomas Aquinas returned to earth today and
circulated amongst men, he would find the most
convincing proof that in man (at least in those of
the left wing) there is something undeniably immortal and unchangeable.

The fact is that it is quite childish on anybody's
part to use the term "betrayal" in such regards or
even to attribute non-intervention policies on the
part of democratic governments to insincerity or
duplicity. Forces quite apart from the individual

consciences of ministers and rulers are in play. For one thing, at critical moments in history, sentiments of class or dynasty readily prevail over affinities of principles, and instinct warns anyone who is in control of a state that one may know how a revolution is to begin but never where or how it is to end, and that in any case revolution is a bad example to set for one's people. Even in extreme cases, when courageous revolutionaries hold the seats of power, they perceive that when the vital interests of their country are at stake, the policy of the state, precisely because it is a state and not a party, must be determined by considerations far other than the theoretical preferences of its ministers or commissars of the people. They see that if they are to stay in power, they must become statesmen and follow state, rather than party, policies. The partisan or theoretical principles, therefore, on which they were carried to power gradually drop into the background ; and instead of the state's being used to apply the utopian principles of a party, we find the party being used to achieve the traditional purposes of the state.

There is apparently something about exiles that renders them impervious to the great political truth just stated. Exiles today, like the exiles of a century ago, keep looking to intervention from abroad for the freeing of their countries ; and whenever what they judge to be a propitious opportunity for

an intervention comes and is missed, they feel themselves "betrayed." And betrayed they are — but
only by their own political education.

Mazzini became an exile in 1830, but it is note-
worthy that he for one showed himself immune to
the weakness just described. To be sure, he denounced French non-interventionist policy as a
"cold, abject, cowardly doctrine," as "atheism applied to international politics," as "the deification, if
one prefer, of selfishness." But this aversion to
non-interventionism was not based on any desire to
see the revolution in Italy, for instance, carried
through by France. "The tree of liberty," he wrote
and often repeated, "bears fruit only when it has
been planted by the hands of citizens, has been
watered with the blood of citizens, and is fenced
about by the courage of citizens." He did not ask
the democratic countries to force democracy by
arms upon the countries still subject to absolutisms.
He did want them to prevent the absolutist states
from interfering to restore to their thrones sovereigns who had been dethroned by popular upris-
ings. Mazzini's "Young Italy," therefore, was an
effort to rescue the democratic movement in Europe from the tutelage of Paris and to distinguish it
sharply from the Revolutionary-Napoleonic tradition in France. Its basic conception was that a
liberation is truly a liberation only when it rises

from the people and that every liberation must be an auto-liberation.

Mazzini wrote a "General Instruction" for "Young Italy" to which every new member of the society had to subscribe. "Convinced," it declared, "that Italy is able to win her independence with her own resources, that a nationality can be founded only when a people is conscious of its nationality, and that such a consciousness cannot be created when an insurrection is carried through to triumph by foreign arms ; convinced furthermore that an insurrection that rests on foreign support depends on the vicissitudes of the foreign country and can therefore never be certain of victory, 'Young Italy' is resolved to take advantage of events in other countries but not to have the time and the character of the revolt dependent on them." No better or more genuine slogan than that could be devised for any revolutionary movement : "Take advantage of everything ; compromise with no one."

VIII

"Mazzini," says Salvemini, "should be counted among the forerunners of present-day socialism, along with Saint Simon, Fourier, Leroux, Pequer, and other humanitarians of the first half of the nineteenth century." Frequent, in fact, in Mazzini's writings are references to the social question, to the need of discovering — perhaps by adopting the suggestions of Saint Simon or the latter's disciples — an economic system under which capital and labor could be associates rather than enemies. The important thing in Mazzini's eye was to prevent economic conflicts from diverting the attention of the citizen from ideal questions. It was imperative, therefore, to remove the causes of poverty, to raise the general standard of living somewhat, to enable frugal and intelligent members of the masses to own property, to open credit to such of the working people as gave evidence of ability, perseverance, and sound morals.

There was nothing extraordinary about that program ; and whenever, furthermore, Mazzini came to view the social question in broad historical perspective, his imagination soared to the clouds on the wings of his conception of a limitless progress developing by stages : "The emancipation of the slave was followed by the emancipation of the serf. The next step will be the emancipation of the proletariat. Progress in human intelligence overthrew the privilege of despotic monarchy through the instrumentality of the patriciate. The privilege of hereditary nobility was overthrown by the bourgeoisie and the aristocracy of money. The people, the laboring masses, will next overthrow the privilege of the property owning and capitalistic bourgeoisie.

When that has come to pass we shall have a society based on labor which will recognize no privilege except the privilege of high-minded intelligence as designated by the choice of an educated, enlightened citizenry to develop talents and social forces."

Mazzini was represented by delegates at the meetings of the First International in London, and in those early days it was not very difficult for the various opposing factions to arrive at compromises. Karl Marx drew up the inaugural statement of outlook and, with his tongue in his cheek we may be sure, inserted a number of sentences to satisfy Mazzini, as for instance the recommendation that the workers "unite all over the world in a simultaneous and public accusation, in order to proclaim the simple principles of morality and right that should govern individual relations, as well as the higher laws that should govern international relations." However, in view of the wide divergences and basic incompatibilities between the three leading schools in ideals, methods, temperaments, and theories, conflict between Mazzinians, Bakuninites, and Marxists could not be long delayed. Marx and Bakunin tried to postpone an open break with Mazzini for a time, in order to have leisure to establish contacts with the Mazzinian groups in Italy and wean them from the master's influence. That tactic was on the whole successful and it was a deadly blow for Mazzini ; for he lost his support among the laboring masses in the Italian towns at the very moment when "Young Italy" was being deserted by middle-class elements in favor of Cavour's unification movements centring around the dynasty of Savoy.

This new alignment corresponded to a far-reaching re-polarization of social and political forces that took place all over Europe between 1848 and 1851. As a result of that transformation one group of forces concentrated around the ownership and control of money, business, and land ; while another group centred about a rising proletariat, which Bakunin, Marx, Blanqui, and their followers were urging to draw apart from other classes, ignore problems of nation and state, and make ready for an imminent social revolution. Intermediate philosophies straightway lost ground in the field of thought. Humanitarian, moralistic, and reformistic theories now found support neither with capital nor with labor, and lacking any influential following they came to be understood for what in fact they were, mere structures of words and sentiments, abstract and utopian. Indeed, not a few inventors of socialist systems, in horror at the implications of the class struggle as proclaimed in the Communist Manifesto, made common cause with conservatism and reaction. Mazzini, for his part, stiffened rigidly in his national-religious apostolate and argued and stormed with scant effect both against the compromising diplomacy of Cavour that was triumph-

ing in the middle classes and the growing power of
Marx and Bakunin which was sweeping the labor
organizations. As the most casual eye could see at
once, Mazzini was irremediably and completely a
beaten man.

It would be a mistake, however, to find the cause
of his failure in the incoherence of his teachings
from a logical or scientific point of view. Success
in politics never depends on the soundness of one's
theoretical principles. In all periods of history we
see political parties attaining power on the basis of
philosophical and social theories that cannot with-
stand critical analysis. The passing of Mazzinianism was due simply to the fact that Mazzini's slogans
and watchwords, both the true ones and the false
ones, were of no interest whatever to those elements
in the population of Europe on whose support
political success depended. Mazzini had a very
limited acquaintance with the sources from which
Marxism sprang, and he therefore had no adequate
appreciation of the real significance of the budding
proletarian movement and of its profound spiritual
content (even if its leaders had little to say about
spirituality, and perhaps, precisely because they had
little to say about it). All the same, the objections
that Mazzini urged against the communist state of
the future were not seldom very much to the point ;
and so too his criticisms of an economic system
where capitalism is supplanted by a state bureau-

cracy are far from being without pertinence today.
As far as his personal preferences went, Mazzini
advocated an economic organization under which
a few basic industries would be managed by the
state, while the bulk of production would be in the
hands of free associations of producers and con-
sumers. These associations would own all existing
capital and all land. After guaranteeing to all members a common minimum wage adequate for sustain-
ing life, they would distribute the remaining sur-
plus according to the quantity and quality of service
rendered. But Mazzini entered upon such questions for argumentative purposes only. In his eyes
the one important question was the establishment
of republican forms of government on the basis of
national unifications. He could not understand
subordinating national to international questions, nor
interests of country to interests of class. "Without
a country," he wrote to the Italian workers, "you
have no name, no identity, no voice, no rights, no
membership in the brotherhood of nations — you remain just the bastards of humanity. Soldiers without a flag, Jews in a world of Gentiles, you will
win neither trust nor protection. You will have
no sponsors. Do not be misled into trying to
achieve your emancipation from an unfair social
condition until you have freed your country. You
will not succeed in such an effort. Only your
country, the blessed land that stretches spacious and

rich between the Alps and the southern rim of
Sicily, can realize your hopes of a better lot." But
of what good would the middle class liberties be
to the working classes ? Mazzini answered : "No
one in Italy, whether he works with his hands or
not, is free to express his thoughts — no one can
have a desire to do so. The press is a monopoly
not of a class but of governments ; and behind the
seven governments of Italy, all more or less avow-
edly hostile to any freedom of thought, stands Austria, hostile to governments, peoples, middle classes,
working classes, thought — to everything that has
an Italian name and semblance. Before the work-
ingman can complain that a freedom won by the
nation is of no advantage to him, the nation must
exist. The seven governments and the Austrian
government must be overthrown."

That was all sound enough ; but the main short-
coming in Mazzini's political outlook was his failure
to perceive the close relationship between the national revolution that was to free the country of
the seven vassal states of Austria and the anti-feudal
revolution that had to take place on the rural estates.
Italy at that time was an economically backward
country. There could be no question of a popular
revolution without the support of the peasantry
which was the main prop of the Church and of the
Austrian domination. Bakunin pointed this out to
Mazzini during one of their talks in London and

Mazzini answered : "For the time being nothing can be done in rural Italy." For that matter, the only reforms in which the Italian peasants could have been interested were not the ones that Mazzini had been preaching. "Illiterate, desperately poor," writes Nello Rosselli, "our peasants were in no position to appreciate the advantages of a moral nature, the promises of new growth, the hopes of a sound but distant economic future which national unity was gradually preparing. They were conscious only of the immediate hardships and discomforts which the new order was causing in the narrow field of their interests. It was easy, therefore, in the general discontent, for the supporters of the dethroned regimes to exploit the animosities of the peasants in organizing a broadly based popular demand for a general restoration. The peasants in the south were the first to react against the new national kingdom, and the reaction took the form of brigandage."

It should be noted, however, that the Marxian socialists erred quite as seriously as Mazzini in their conception of the relations of the social question to the national question, of the economic revolution to the social revolution. They succeeded indeed in eventually winning a large following among factory hands and day laborers on the farms by obtaining very considerable improvements in conditions of living. But those gains were very precarious and short-lived since they were not protected and re-enforced by a thoroughgoing democratization of the country ; and the neglect of political reforms and indifference to forms of government that were very general in socialist propaganda contributed very considerably later on to the Fascist counter-revolution.

Ignazio Silone has selected and arranged
the essence of Mazzini's thought from

THE COMPLETE
EDITION OF MAZZINI'S WRITINGS

THE WORKS OF
GIUSEPPE MAZZINI
(1805–1872)

Thoughts upon Democracy in Europe
On the Duties of Man
Central Europe (journal)
Popular Apostleship (journal)
Thought and Action (journal)
Letters

I

THE CALL

It was during these months of imprisonment in Savona that I conceived the plan of the association of Young Italy (*La Giovina Italia*). I meditated deeply upon the principles upon which to base the organisation of the party, the aim and purpose of its labours — which I intended should be publicly declared — the method of its formation, the individuals to be selected to aid me in its creation, and the possibility of linking its operations with those of the existing revolutionary elements of Europe.

We were few in number, young in years, and of limited means and influence; but I believed the whole problem to consist in appealing to the true instincts and tendencies of the Italian heart, mute at that time, but revealed to us both by history and our own previsions of the future. Our strength must lie in our right appreciation of what those instincts and tendencies really were.

All great national enterprises have ever been originated by men of the people, whose sole strength lay in that power of *faith* and of *will*, which neither counts obstacles nor measures time. Men of means and influence follow after, either to support and carry on the movement created by the first, or, as too often happens, to divert it from its original aim.

I was not influenced by any mere political conception, nor idea of elevating the condition of the single people whom I saw thus dismembered, degraded, and oppressed ; the parent thought of my every design was a presentiment that regenerated Italy was destined to arise the *initiatrix* of a new life, and a new and powerful Unity to all the nations of Europe.

Even at that time, in spite of the fascination exercised over my mind by the fervid words in which France at that day asserted her right of leadership amid the general silence, the idea was dimly stirring within me to which I gave expression six years later — the sense of a void, a want in Europe.

I felt that authority — true righteous and holy authority — the search after which, whether conscious or not, is in fact the secret of our human life, and which is only irrationally denied by those who confound it with its false semblance or shadow, and imagine they have abolished God himself, when they have but abolished an idol ; — I felt that authority had vanished, and become extinct in Europe ; and that for this reason no power of *initiative* existed in any of the peoples of Europe.

The labours, studies, and sorrows of my life have not only justified and confirmed this idea, but have transformed it into a *faith*. And if ever — though I may not think it — I should live to see Italy One, and to pass one year of solitude in some corner of my own land, or of this land where I now write, and which affection has rendered a second country to me, I shall endeavour to develope and reduce the consequences which flow from this idea, and are of far greater importance than most men believe.

At that time even the immature conception inspired me with a mighty hope that flashed before my spirit like a star. I saw regenerate Italy becoming at one bound the missionary of a religion of progress and fraternity, far grander and vaster than that she gave to humanity in the past.

The worship of Rome was a part of my being. The great Unity, the One Life of the world, had twice been elaborated within her walls. Other peoples — their brief mission fulfilled — disappeared for ever. To none save to her had it been given twice to guide and direct the world. There, life was eternal, death unknown. There, upon the vestiges of an epoch of civilisation anterior to the Grecian, which had had its seat in Italy, and which the historical science of the future will show to have had a far wider external influence than the learned of our own day imagine — the Rome of the Republic, concluded by the Cæsars, had arisen to consign the former world to oblivion, and borne her eagles over the known world, carrying with them the idea of right, the source of liberty.

In later days, while men were mourning over her as the sepulchre of the living, she had again arisen, greater than before, and at once constituted herself, through her Popes — as venerable once as abject now — the accepted centre of a new Unity, elevating the law from earth to heaven, and substituting to the idea of right an idea of duty — a duty common to all men, and therefore source of their equality.

Why should not a new Rome, the Rome of the Italian people — portents of whose coming I deemed I saw — arise to create a third and still vaster unity ; to link together and harmonize earth and heaven, right and duty ; and utter, not to individuals but to peoples, the great word Association — to make known to free men and equals their mission here below ?

The immediate result of these ideas was to convince me that the labour to be undertaken was not merely a political, but above all a moral work ; not negative, but religious ; not founded upon any theory of self-interest, or well-being, but upon principles and upon duty.

During the first months of my university life my mind had been somewhat tainted by the doctrines of the foreign materialist school ; but the study of history and the intuition of conscience — the only tests of truth — soon led me back to the spiritualism of our Italian fathers.

II

THE CARBONARI AND THE LIBERAL
UPRISINGS OF 1831

Carbonarism appeared to me to be simply a vast *liberal* association, in the sense in which the word was used in France during the monarchies of Louis XVIII and Charles X, but condemned by the absence of a fixed and determinate belief to lack the power of unity, without which success in any great enterprise is impossible.

Arising during the period when the gigantic but tyrannous Napoleonic unity was tottering to its fall, amid the ruins of a world ; amid the strife between young hopes and old usurpations ; and the dim foreshadowings of the people opposed to the records of a past the governments were seeking to revive ; — Carbonarism bore the stamp of all these diverse elements, and appeared in doubtful form amid the darkness diffused over Europe at that critical period.

The royal protection it encountered at its outset, and indeed so long as there were hopes of using it as an instrument of warfare against imperial France, had contributed to give the institution an uncertain method of action which tended to divert men's minds from the national aim. True it is that on seeing itself betrayed it had cast off the yoke, but

preserving unconsciously some of its former habits,
and above all a fatal tendency to seek its chiefs in
the highest spheres of society, and to regard the
regeneration of Italy rather as the business of the
superior classes than as the duty of the people, sole
creators of great revolutions. It was a vital error,
but inevitable in every political body wanting a
sound religious faith in a great and fruitful principle, supreme over all the changes of passing
events.

Now Carbonarism had no such principle. Its
only weapon was a mere negation. It called upon
men to overthrow : it did not teach them how to
build up a new edifice upon the ruins of the old.

The chiefs of the Order, while studying the national problem, had discovered that although all the
Italians were agreed upon the question of independence, they were not so upon the question of
unity, nor even upon the meaning to be attached to
the word liberty.

Alarmed at this difficulty, and incapable of de-
ciding between the different parties, they chose a
middle path, and inscribed *Liberty* and *Independence* upon their banner. They did not define what
they understood by liberty, nor declare how they
intended to achieve it : the country, they said —
and by the country they meant the upper classes —
the country will decide at a future day.

In the same spirit they substituted the word *union*

to that of *unity*, thus leaving the field open to every hypothesis.

Of equality they either did not speak, or in so vague a manner as to allow every man to interpret it according to his own views, as political, civil, or merely Christian equality.

Thus did the Carbonari begin their work of affiliation, without affording any satisfactory issue to the doubts and questions then agitating men's minds, and without informing those whom they summoned to the struggle what programme they had to offer to the people in return for the support expected from them.

And numerous recruits were enrolled from all classes ; for in all there were numerous malcontents, who desired no better than to prepare the overthrow of the existing order of things ; and also because the profound mystery in which the smallest acts of the Order were enveloped exercised a great fascination over the imagination of the Italians, always impressionable to excess.

A sense of its being necessary to satisfy the tastes of the immense body of members composing the various grades of their complex and intricate hierarchy, had suggested the adoption of a variety of strange and incomprehensible symbols which concealed the absence of any real doctrine or principle. But they were in fact rather used to protect the hierarchy from inquisition than adopted with a view to action ; and hence the orders of the chiefs were feebly and tardily obeyed. The severity of discipline was more apparent than real.

The society had, however, reached a degree of numerical strength unknown to any of the societies by which it was succeeded. But the Carbonari did not know how to turn their strength to account. Although the doctrines of Carbonarism were widely diffused, its leaders had no confidence in the people ; and appealed to them rather to attain an appearance of force likely to attract those men of rank and station in whom alone they put their trust, than from any idea of leading them to immediate action.

Hence the ardour and energy of the youth of the Order — of those who dreamed only of country, the republic, war, and glory in the eyes of Europe — was entrusted to the direction of men, not only old in years, but imbued with the ideas of the empire ; cold precisionists, who had neither faith nor future, and who, instead of fostering, repressed all daring and enthusiasm.

At a later period, when the immense mass of Carbonari already affiliated, and the consequent impossibility of preserving secrecy, convinced the leaders of the necessity for action, they felt the want of some stronger bond of unity ; and not having a *principle* upon which to found it, they set themselves to seek it in a *man — a prince*.

This was the ruin of Carbonarism.

Intellectually the Carbonari were materialist and Machiavellian. They preached the doctrine of political liberty; yet the literary men among them, forgetting that man is one, taught literary servitude under the name of *classicism*. They called themselves Christians in their symbolic language; yet, confounding religion with the Papacy, and faith with superstition, they contrived to wither up the virgin enthusiasm of youth by a scepticism borrowed from Voltaire, and the negations of the eighteenth century. They were mere sectarians, not the apostles of a national religion.

Such were they also in the sphere of politics. They had no sincere faith in the constitutional form of government; they sneered at monarchy among themselves, yet nevertheless they hailed and supported it; at first as a means of acquiring strength, afterwards because the adoption of the monarchical system freed them from the responsibility of guiding the masses whom they feared and misunderstood; and at last because they hoped by baptizing the insurrection with a royal name, to soften Austria, and win the favour of some great power — either England or France.

It was for this reason they cast their eyes on Charles Albert in Piedmont, and Prince Francesco at Naples; the first a man of a tyrannical nature, and though ambitious, incapable of greatness; the second a hypocrite and traitor from the very be-

ginning of his career. They offered the management of the destinies of Italy to each of these
princes, leaving it to the future to arrange the irreconcilable views of the two pretenders.

Events, however, clearly proved that true
strength is derived not from the mass, but from the
cohesion of the elements by which the aim is to
be achieved; and revealed the inevitable consequences of the absence of principles in those who
place themselves at the head of revolutions.

The insurrections of the Carbonari were successful — they had no very grave difficulties to overcome; — but they were immediately followed by
serious internal discord. The work of mere destruction once fulfilled, each Carbonaro fell back
upon his own individual aims and opinions, and all
were at variance as to what they had to create.
Some had imagined themselves to be conspiring in
the interest of a single monarchy; many were parti-
zans of the French constitution, many of the Spanish; some were for a republic; others for I know
not how many republics; and all of these com-
plained that they had been deceived.

The Provisional Governments were weakened
therefore, at the very outset, by the open opposition
of some, and the studied inertia of others. Hence
the hesitation and uncertainty manifested by those
governments who found a pretext for inactivity in

that opposition to which action alone could have put an end. Hence, the youthful volunteers and the people were left without encouragement, organisation, or definite aim.

All true liberty in the selection of means was rendered impossible by the fact of the monarchy having been chosen leader of the revolution ; as it naturally brought along with it a host of traditions and obligations, all hostile to the daring development of the insurrectionary principle.

Logic will ever assert its rights. The chiefs of the movement, having implicitly declared the people incapable of either emancipating or governing themselves, necessarily abstained from arming them, or inducing them to take any share in the management of affairs. It was equally necessary to substitute some other force to that of the people, and to seek this force abroad, from foreign cabinets ; to obtain false promises in return for real concessions ; and to allow the princes free choice both of their ministers and generals, even at the risk — as shown in the sequel — of their selecting the treacherous or incapable, and of seeing the princes themselves suddenly desert to the enemy's camp, or fly to Laybach, thence to cry anathema upon the insurrection they had feigned to conduct.

Such did Carbonarism appear to me — a huge and powerful body, but without a head ; an association in which not generous intentions, but ideas, were wanting ; deficient in the science and logic which should have reduced the sentiment of nationality, pervading its ranks, to fruitful action.

The *cosmopolitanism* of the Carbonari, suggested by the superficial study of foreign countries, while it had extended the Order's sphere of action, had yet withdrawn the fulcrum of the lever.

The lesson of heroic constancy taught by the Carbonari, and the boldness with which they had fronted martyrdom, had tended greatly to promote that sentiment of equality which is innate in us Italians, and prepared the way for union and noble enterprise, by initiating in one sole baptism men of every province, and of every social class — priests, nobles, literary men, soldiers, and sons of the people.

But the absence of a definite programme had always caused victory to escape them at the very moment when it was within their grasp.

These reflections were suggested to me by an examination of the various attempts made by the Carbonari, and their defeats. And recent events in central Italy had confirmed me in my ideas, besides pointing out to me other dangers to be avoided ; foremost among which were the fatal habit of founding the hope of victory upon the support of foreign governments, and that of confiding the management and development of the insurrection to men who had had no share in creating it.

The revolution of 1831 revealed an unquestionable progress in the political education of the insurgents. That insurrection neither invoked the initiative of the higher classes, nor of the military, as indispensable ; it burst out among men of no name, and from the true heart of the country.

After the three days of Paris, the post-office at Bologna was crowded and surrounded by the people. Young men stood up on the benches in front of the cafés, and read the newspapers aloud to the bystanders. Arms were got ready, companies of volunteers were organised, and captains chosen. The commandant declared to the prolegate that the troops would not act against the citizens. Similar scenes took place in many other cities.

The revolution — from the very nature of its elements, and the special position of the provinces in insurrection — was necessarily republican ; the sympathy of existing governments was therefore impossible, and it became urgent to seek allies in the homogeneous element, among the peoples.

The sole pledge of alliance among peoples is a declaration of principles. They made no such declaration ; they sought the favour of kings, and prostrated the movement of the peoples at the feet of diplomacy.

It was necessary to excite to action by acting themselves ; to awaken energy by displaying energy ; to rouse faith by showing faith : and they, by their weakness and hesitation, betrayed their fears in every act. Hence, a sense of distrust arose in the insurgent states, and discouragement spread over the other provinces of Italy. Hence diplomatic treachery, and the unavoidable ruin of the whole movement.

The principle of non-intervention had, it is true, been explicitly and solemnly proclaimed by the French Government. Before the insurrection took place, a memorial had been drawn up by various influential Italians to inquire of the French Ambassador at Naples (Latour Maubourg) what would be the conduct of France in case an Italian revolution should provoke the armed intervention of Austria, and the Ambassador had written on the margin, with his own hand, that "France would support the revolution, provided the new government should not assume an anarchical form, and should recognise the order of things generally adopted in Europe."

Latour Maubourg afterwards denied this note, which was, however, sent to the Provisional Government during the first days of the movement. One of the members of that government, Francesco Orioli, who saw it, has attested the fact in his work,

De la Revolution d'Italie, printed in Paris in 1834–35.

Moreover, Lafitte, then President of the Chamber of Deputies, had spoken the following words on the 1st December 1830 : "France will not allow any violation of the principle of non-intervention. . . The Holy Alliance made it a fundamental principle to suffocate popular liberty wheresoever it should raise its standard ; the new principle proclaimed by France is that of allowing the unimpeded development of liberty wheresoever it may spontaneously arise."

On the 15th of January, Guizot had declared, "The principle of non-intervention is identical with the principle of the liberty of the peoples" ; and on the 22d of the same month, the Minister of Foreign Affairs had said, "The Holy Alliance was founded on the principle of intervention for the overthrow of the independence of all secondary states ; the opposite principle, consecrated by us, and which we intend to see respected, assures liberty and independence to all."

On the 28th the same things were repeated by the Duke of Dalmatia, and on the 29th by Sebastiani.

But if the leaders of the movement had, therefore, reason to believe that they should not be betrayed, it was nevertheless their duty to remember that, at that time (1831), any war between France and

Austria would have certainly resolved itself into a general war between the principle of immobility and that of progress and national sovereignty ; and that in such a war, though France herself would have reaped nothing but triumph, Louis Philippe would have run the risk of losing everything, and being overwhelmed by the popular movement.

The French monarchy was weak, and utterly destitute of all support from popular sympathy. A revolutionary impulse given to France might have dragged it into the vortex of a war which, from the nature of the elements brought into play, would probably have rapidly assumed the character of a republican crusade. Peace was therefore necessary to the very existence of the dynasty.

There was only one means of compelling the French monarchy to maintain its promises — viz., to contrive to hold out long enough to rouse the sympathy of public opinion in France, and to use every exertion to extend the movement on every side, especially in Piedmont, wherein the intervention of Austria, like that of Prussia in Belgium, is irreconcilable with the traditionary policy of France.

The idea of overcoming the repugnance of Louis Philippe by a display of weakness was absolute madness, as it was madness to imagine that any principle of non-intervention would interfere with the advance of Austria. Even at the risk of war, Austria could not allow the establishment of a free govern-

ment in the vicinity of her Lombardo-Venetian pos-
sessions.

Thus the Insurrectionary Government, by neg-
lecting to make preparations for war, while it gave
Austria time enough to come to a rapid settlement
of all her dissensions with France, yet left no time
for the French Liberals to create a public opinion
in their favour.

The importance of the question of time was so
well understood by Louis Philippe, that, trusting the
insurrection might be suppressed before he should
be called upon to give an account of his promises,
he concealed the arrival of the dispatch of the
French Ambassador at Vienna announcing the invasion of Central Italy by Austria, and withheld it
for five days from the honest but incapable Lafitte,
then President of the Council.

However, the Provisional Governments of the insurgent provinces chose to adopt the hypothesis that
Austria would not invade, that she would allow the
insurrection time enough to implant itself firmly in
the heart of Italy, and decided that the whole policy of the revolution ought therefore to consist in
avoiding giving any just ground for invasion.

Not a single act was passed, therefore, asserting
the sovereignty and right of the nation ; none to call
the people to arms ; none to organise the elections ;
none to incite or encourage the neighbouring provinces of Italy to rise.

Fear was visible in their every decree.

The revolution was made to appear a thing accepted rather than asserted and proclaimed.

This unlimited confidence in everything bearing the outward semblance of calculation and tactics, and this constant distrust of all enthusiasm, energy, and simultaneous action — three things which sum up the whole science of revolution — was then, as it is now, the mortal disease of Italy. We wait, study, and follow circumstances ; we neither seek to dominate nor create them. We honour with the name of prudence that which is, in act, merely mediocrity of intellect.

From studying the ill-fated movements of 1820–21 and 1831, I learned what errors it would be necessary to avoid in future. The greater number of Italians — who did not pause to distinguish between the events themselves and the men who attempted to control them — derived from these insurrections only a lesson of profound discouragement.

To me they simply brought the conviction that success was a problem of *direction*, nothing more. Others opined that the blame I bestowed upon the directors of the movements, ought to fall upon the whole country. The mere fact that such men rather than others had risen to power, was considered very generally to be the result of a vice inherent in the condition of Italy ; and as giving an average — so to speak — of the Italian revolutionary power. I merely regarded that choice as a fault of logic, easily to be remedied.

That error was the error only too prevalent at the present day — that of entrusting the government of the Insurrection to those who had had no share in making it.

The people and the youth of Italy have always yielded the reins of direction to the first man claiming the right to hold them with any show of authority. This may be traced to a well-meant but over-strained desire of legality, and an honourable though exaggerated fear of being accused of anarchy or ambition ; to a traditionary habit, useful only in a normal state of things, of trusting to men of advanced age, or local influence ; and to their absolute inexperience of the nature and development of great revolutions.

The preliminary conspiracy and the revolution have always been represented by two distinct classes of men. The first were thrust aside as soon as all obstacles were overthrown, and the others then entered the arena the day after, to direct the development of an idea not their own, a design they had not matured, the elements and difficulties of which they had never studied, and in the enthusiasm and sacrifices of which they had had no share.

Thus in Piedmont, in 1821, the development of

the revolutionary idea was confided to men who, like Dal Pozzo,* Villamarina, and Gubernatis, had been entire strangers to the preliminary conspiracy.

Thus, in Bologna, they had accepted as members of their Provisional Government men who were approved by the government overthrown ; men whose title to office was derived from an edict of Monsignore Clarelli. Thus the councils of commercial administration, having assumed the name of civil congresses, had declared themselves the legal representatives of the people, and without a shadow of right proceeded to elect the provisional authorities.

Now, the majority in these councils was composed of grey-headed men, educated under the old system of ideas, distrustful of the young, and still under the influence of the terror inspired by the excesses of the French Revolution.

Their liberalism was like that of the party called *moderate* in Italy at the present day ; weak and fearful ; capable of a timid legal opposition on points of detail, but never going back to first principles.

They naturally elected men similarly constituted, descendants of the old families, professors, advocates with many clients, but all of them men disinherited alike of the enthusiasm, energy, or intellect necessary to achieve revolutions.

Our young men, trustful and inexperienced, gave

* Dal Pozzo, when driven into exile in 1821, obtained permission to return by selling his pen to Austria.

way. They forgot the immense difference between the wants of a free and of an enslaved people, and the improbability that the same men who had represented the individual and municipal interests of the last, should be fitted to represent the political and national interests of the first.

III

OUTLOOK MORAL AND POLITICAL

The instructions which, in that first period of the association, I continued to impart to the various committees and directors, as well as the other young Italians with whom I came in contact, were both moral and political.

The following is a summary of the bearing of the moral instructions:

"We are not only conspirators, but believers.

"We aspire to be not only revolutionists; but, so far as we may, regenerators.

"Our problem is, above all things, a problem of national education. Arms and insurrection are merely the means without which, in the position of our country, it is impossible to solve that problem. But we will only use bayonets on the condition that they have ideas at their points.

"It were of little import to destroy, if we had not the hope of building up something better; of little use to write duty and right upon a fragment of paper, if we had not the firm determination and the faith that we can engrave them upon men's hearts.

"Our fathers neglected to do this, therefore it is our duty ever to bear it in mind. It is not enough to persuade the various states of Italy to rise in insurrection. What we have to do is to create a nation.

"It is our religious conviction that Italy has not consumed her life in this world. She is yet destined to introduce new elements in the progressive development of humanity, and to live a third life. Our object is to endeavour to initiate this life.

"Materialism can generate no political doctrine but that of *individuality* — a doctrine useful, perhaps, if supported by force, in securing the exercise of some personal rights, but impotent to found nationality or association ; both of which require faith in our unity of origin, of tendency, and of aim. We reject it.

"We must endeavour to take up the thread of the Italian philosophy of the sixteenth and seventeenth centuries ; to carry on its tradition of synthesis and spirituality ; to rekindle a strong and earnest faith ; and, by re-awakening the consciousness of the great deeds of their nation in the hearts of the Italians, to inspire them with the courage, power of sacrifice, constancy, and concord, necessary for our great work."

The political instructions declared :

"The most logical party is ever the strongest. Do not be satisfied with inspiring a mere spirit of rebellion in your followers, nor an uncertain indefinite declaration of liberalism. Ask of each man in what he believes, and only accept as members those whose convictions are the same as our own. Put your trust, not so much in the number, as in the unity of your forces.

"Ours is an experiment upon the Italian people. We may resign ourselves to the possibility of seeing our hopes betrayed, but we may not risk the danger of seeing discord arise in the camp the day after action.

"You have to elevate a new banner, and you must seek its supporters among the young, who are capable of enthusiasm, energy, and sacrifice. Tell them the whole truth. Let them know all as to our aim and intent. We can then rely upon them if they accept it.

"The great error of the past has been that of intrusting the fate of the country to individuals rather than to principles.

"Combat this error, and preach faith, not in names but in the people, in our rights, and in God.

"Teach your followers that they must choose their leaders among men who seek their inspiration from revolution, not from the previous order of things. Lay bare all the errors committed in 1831, and do not conceal the faults of the leaders.

"Repeat incessantly that the salvation of Italy lies in her people. The lever of the people is action, continuous action ; action ever renewed, without allowing one's self to be overcome or disheartened by first defeats.

"Avoid compromises. They are almost always immoral, as well as dangerous.

"Do not deceive yourselves with any idea of the possibility of avoiding war, a war both bloody and inexorable, with Austria. Seek rather, as soon as you feel you are strong enough, to promote it. Revolutionary war should always take the offensive. By being the first to attack, you inspire your enemies with terror, and your friends with courage and confidence.

"Hope nothing from foreign governments. They will never be really willing to aid you until you have shown that you are strong enough to conquer without them.

"Put no trust in diplomacy, but disconcert its intrigues by beginning the struggle, and by publicity in all things.

"Never rise in any other name than that of Italy, and of all Italy. If you gain your first battle in the name of a principle, and with your own forces alone, it will give you the position of initiators among the peoples, and you will have them for companions in the second. And should you fall, you will at least have helped to educate your countrymen, and leave behind you a programme to direct the generation to come."

Many of those who were in contact with me at that time are still living, and can bear witness that the above is the true tenor of my instructions.

The experiment succeeded. The *soi-disant* thinkers of that day were confuted by the people.

IV

NATIONALITY AND NATIONALISMS : TACTIC
FOR SWITZERLAND

The age that has just passed, the age that ended with the French Revolution, performed a mission, the mission of emancipating man as an individual, providing him with three dogmas, the dogmas of liberty, equality and fraternity. The era that is now dawning will have the task of organising humanity, in other words, socialism, not only in its individual applications but as between people and people — it will have the task of organising a Europe of free peoples, independent as regards their domestic functioning, mutually associated with one another as regards their common outlook — and the motto will be : "Liberty, Equality, Humanity."

Hitherto France has been in the lead. In '89 France assumed full direction of the process of civilising Europe. All initiative in the movement has been taken by France exclusively. Now the time has come when the exclusive supremacy of a single people must disappear through the rehabilitation of all peoples, through the specification of new missions. Each people will have its mission and that mission will constitute its test of nationality. From the harmonious interplay of these special missions will derive the general mission of all peoples : Progress toward Humanity !

This theory of ours, which is the idea of "Young Europe," should be welcomed with very special favour in Switzerland, since it is our aim to make of that country a nation, to find a place for her among the elements of European civilisation, to provide her with a mission. Hitherto, one has to confess, Switzerland has given no signs of awareness of any mission. Insignificant, weak, wavering back and forth between France and Austria, she has counted for nothing in the great European equilibrium. She has been a despised plaything for the tyrants, and at present she is threatened with even worse. If she is not resigned to being the first victim in the next European crisis she has to bestir herself, come to life, find a purpose, a faith, a religion of principles, as regards both domestic and foreign relations.

Her purposes at home must be fixed by a constituent assembly, a truly national assembly, that will annul the outworn pact of 1815 and replace it with something more national. Abroad, her resolve must be to unite in ties of brotherhood with the peoples who are determined to be free. This alliance will replace the old league of governments. The mission that Switzerland must fulfill abroad I intend to define in a pamphlet that I shall shortly be publishing in Switzerland. Meantime the task is to prepare the ground that the seed we are to sow may fall on fertile soil. We must drive the idea of "Young Europe" in ! We must make it plain that "Young Europe" is not a sect but an association, that its aim is not merely destructive, but more particularly and more importantly constructive. We must emphasise the fact that "Young Europe" is not merely promoting a political idea but is giving religious status to a principle of regeneration that is to find its application in all departments of human endeavour. "Young Europe" is creating a new philosophy, a new literature, a new political economy. Coming down to more immediate and specific concerns we must suggest that great events are in the offing, events, which, whenever they may materialise, will necessarily bring on a European war and a world war, since principles are involved. The absolute governments will surely try to take advantage of this coming opportunity to stamp out the Swiss form of republican government and accomplish at last the long hoped-for dismemberment of Switzerland. Only one thing can prevent this catastrophe, a league of peoples, a league of freemen of all countries — "Young Europe" in short !

V

POLICIES OF PRINCIPLES AND POLICIES OF INTEREST ?

You deceive yourselves, we are told. The peoples lack faith. The masses are dormant, inert. They have worn chains so long as to lose the habit of motion. You have to do with Helots, not with men. How can you drag them into the battle, or maintain them in the field? How often have we called them to arms to the cry of *people, liberty, vengeance!* They did but raise their heavy heads for an instant, to sink back into their former stupor. They have seen the funeral procession of our martyrs pass them by, and understood not that with them were entombed their own rights, their own lives, their own salvation. They seek after gold, and are held in inertia by fear. Enthusiasm is extinct, and it is not easy to rekindle it. Now, without the help of the masses you cannot act; you may reach martyrdom, but not victory. Die, if you believe that your blood will sooner or later raise up a generation of avengers, but do not seek to drag into your destiny those who have neither your energy nor your hopes. Martyrdom can never become the religion of a whole party. It is useless to exhaust the forces which may one day be of service in unsuccessful efforts. Do not deceive yourselves as to your epoch. Resign yourselves to await in patience.

The question is momentous. It involves the future of the party.

Yes, the peoples lack faith : not that individual faith which creates martyrs, but that *social* faith which is the parent of victory ; the faith that arouses the multitudes ; faith in their own destiny, in their own mission, and in the mission of the epoch : the faith that combats and prays ; the faith that enlightens, and bids men advance fearlessly in the ways of God and Humanity, with the sword of the people in their hand, the religion of the people in their heart, and the future of the people in their soul.

But such faith as this — preached by the sole priest of the Epoch, Lamennais — and which we are all bound *nationally* to reduce to action — what is wanted to give it to us ? Is it strength, or the consciousness of strength, that we need ? Have we lost it through the recognition of our real powerlessness, or through opinions that are erroneous, and prejudices that may be removed ? Would not one energetic act of will re-establish an equilibrium between the oppressor and the oppressed ? And suppose this to be so, have we striven to achieve it ? Are our own tendencies, our own manifestations of the idea we seek to promote, such as to realise the aim? Are we, whom chance has placed at the head of the movement, or are the multitudes who do but follow lead, to blame for the actual state of inertia?

Look at Italy. Misfortune, suffering, protest, individual sacrifice, have reached their climax there. The cup is full. Oppression is everywhere, like the air we breathe, but rebellion also. Three separate states, twenty cities, two millions of men arise, and in one week overthrow their governments, and proclaim their own emancipation, without a single protest raised, or a single drop of blood shed. One attempt constantly succeeds another. Do these twenty-five millions of men lack strength? Italy in revolution would be strong enough to conquer three Austrias. Do they lack the inspiration of great traditions — the religion of memory — the past? The people still bow down in reverence before the relics of the grandeur that has been. Do they lack a mission? Only to Italy has it been vouchsafed twice to give the word of unity to Europe. Do they lack courage? Ask it of 1746, of the records of the Grande Armée? of the thrice holy martyrs who, during the last fourteen years, have died there silently, without glory, for an idea.

Look at Switzerland. Can anyone deny the valour or the profound spirit of independence that distinguishes these sons of the Alps? Five centuries of struggle, of intrigues, and of civil and religious discord, have failed to soil the Swiss banner of 1308. Nevertheless, Switzerland, whose battle-cry would arouse Germany and Italy, though well aware how the monarchs of Europe would shrink from the idea of an European war sought by the peoples, because conscious that the last battle of that war would be the Waterloo of Monarchy, — Switzerland continually submits to insult and stoops to dishonour at the present day, and bows her head to the paltriest note of an Austrian agent.

Remember 1813 : the youth of Germany abandoning their universities to fight the battles of independence ; the thrill that ran throughout the whole country at the cry of *nationality* and independence ; — and tell me whether that people would not have arisen had their deputies, electors, writers, all the influential men who preferred the circumlocution of constitutional opposition, rallied around the banner of Hambach ?

Remember Grochow, Waver, Ostrolenska ; and tell me what would have been the condition of Russia, if instead of wasting precious time in imploring the protection of diplomacy for that Poland which diplomacy had been sacrificing for a century past, — the combatants had rapidly carried the action of the revolutionary principle to its natural centre, beyond the Bug ; if a vaster conception of popular emancipation had called into action those races whose secret was revealed in 1848 by Bogdan

Chielmicki, — if while enthusiasm reigned supreme and the enemy was stupefied by terror, while the multitudes of Lithuania, Ukrania, and Galicia, were burning with the hope of liberty, the insurrectionary forces had pushed on into Lithuania.

I write it with the deepest conviction : there is scarcely a single people unable by dint of faith, sacrifice, and revolutionary logic, to burst their chains in the face of the monarchies of Europe united against them ; — not a single people who in the holiness of an idea of love and the future, and in the strength of a word inscribed upon their insurrectionary banner, might not initiate an European crusade ; — not a single people to whom the opportunity of doing so has not been offered since 1830.

But in Italy, in Germany, in Poland, in Switzerland, in France, everywhere indeed, the true original nature of the revolutionary movements has been altered by men, unfortunately influential, but grasping and ambitious ; who have regarded the uprising of a people but as an opportunity for power or profit ; — or by weak men, trembling at the difficulties and dangers of the enterprise, who have at the outset sacrificed the logic of insurrection to their own fears. Everywhere have false and pernicious doctrines caused the revolutions to deviate from their true aim ; the idea of a caste has been substituted for the popular idea of the emancipation of all by all ; the idea of foreign help has weakened or de-

stroyed the national idea. Nowhere have the pro-
moters, the leaders, the governments of the insurrections, determined to cast into the balance of the
country's destiny, the entire sum of forces which
might have been put in motion by sufficient energy
of will ; nowhere has the consciousness of a great
mission, and faith in its fulfilment, a true comprehension of the age and of its ruling thought, governed the action of those who, by assuming the
direction of events, had pledged themselves to humanity for their successful issue.

The mission before them was a mission of giants,
and to perform it they stooped down to earth.
They had half divined the secret of the generations ; they had heard the cry of the great human
families striving to shake off the dust of the sepulchre, and to arise to new life ; they were called
upon to declare the Word of the people and of the
peoples, without fear or reserve, — and they did but
stammer forth hesitating words of concessions, of
charters, of compacts between power and right, between the unjust and the just. Even as age in its
decrepitude demands of art some element of facti-
tious life, so they sought from the policy of the past
the *idea* of its imperfect and fugitive existence.
They were bound — even though it were raised
upon their own dead bodies — to elevate the banner of insurrection so high that all the peoples
might read thereon its promise of victory ; and they

dragged it through the mud of royalty, veiled it beneath protocols, or hung it idly up — an ensign of prostitution — over the doors of foreign *Chancelleries*. They put their trust in the promises of every minister, in the hopes held out by every ambassador, in everything save in the omnipotence of the people.

We have seen the leaders of revolution immersed in the study of the treaties of 1815, seeking therein the charter of Italian or Polish liberty : others, more culpable, proclaiming aloud the negation of Humanity, and the affirmation of egotism, by inscribing upon their banner a principle of *non-intervention* worthy of the middle ages : others, more guilty still, denying both their brothers and their fatherland, and breaking the national unity at the very moment when it behoved them to initiate its triumph, when the foreigner was advancing to their gates, by declaring : *Bolognese ! the cause of the Modenese is not our cause.*

In their anxiety to *legalise* their revolution they forgot that every insurrection must derive its legality from its *aim*, its legitimacy from victory, its means of *defence* from *offence*, and the pledge of its success from its extension. They forgot that the charter of a nation's liberties is an article of the charter of humanity, and that they alone deserve that charter who are ready to conquer or die for all humanity.

When the peoples saw the initiators of revolution turn pale before the enterprise, and either shrink from the necessity of action, or advance trembling and uncertain, without any definite purpose, without any programme, or any hope save in foreign aid, even they became timid and hesitating ; or rather they felt that the hour was not yet come, and held back. In the face of revolutions betrayed at their very outset, the multitudes stood aloof ; enthusiasm was crushed at its birth ; faith disappeared.

Faith disappeared : but what have we done, what do we even now to revive it ? Shame and grief ! Ever since that holy light of the peoples faded away, we have either wandered in the darkness, without bond, plan, or unity of design ; or folded our arms like men in despair. Some of us, after uttering a long cry of grief, have renounced all earthly progress to murmur a hymn of resignation, a prayer like the prayer of the dying : others have rebelled against hope, and, smiling in bitterness, have proclaimed the reign of darkness by accepting scepticism, irony, and incredulity as things inevitable, and their blasphemy has been responded to by the corruption of those already degraded, and by the suicide or despair of the pure in heart. The literature of the present day oscillates between these two extremes. Others, remembering the light that had illumined their infancy, retraced their weary steps to the sanctuary they had abandoned, hoping to rekindle the flame; or, concentrating the mind in purely subjective contemplation, merged existence in the *Ego*, forgetting or denying the external world to bury themselves in the study of the individual. Such is our present philosophy.

Others, born to struggle, and urged on by a power of sacrifice which, wisely directed, might have wrought miracles — impelled by instincts sublime, but indefinite — seized the banner that floated over the graves of their fathers, and rushed onwards; but they separated before they had advanced many steps, and each of them tearing a fragment from the banner, endeavoured to make of it the standard of the entire army. Such is the history of our political life.

The reader must pardon my reiterating these plaints. They are my *delenda est Carthago*. My work is not a labour of authorship, but a sincere and earnest mission of apostolate. Such a mission does not admit of diplomacy. I am seeking the secret of the delay in our advance, which appears to me to be attributable to causes apart from the strength of the enemy; I am striving to put the question in such a manner as will enable us speedily to regain a lost initiative. I must either be silent or speak out the whole truth.

Now it seems to me that there are two principal causes for this delay ; both of them dependent upon the party's deviation from the true path ; both of them tending to the substitution of the worship of the past for the worship of the future.

The first is the error which has led us to regard as a programme of the future that which was in fact but a grand summing up of the past ; a formula expressing the results of the labour and achievements of an entire epoch — to confound two distinct epochs and two distinct syntheses — and to narrow a mission of social renovation to the proportions of a mere work of deduction and development. It has led us to abandon the principle for the symbol, the God for the idol ; to immobilise that *initiative* which is the cross of fire transmitted by God from people to people ; to destroy the legitimacy of nationality, which is the life of the peoples, their mission, and the means given them by which to achieve it ; which marks out the part assigned to them by God in our common work and duty — the evolution of His thought, one and multiple, which is the soul of our existence here below.

The second cause is the error which has led us to confound the principle with one of its manifestations; the eternal element of every social organisation with one of its successive developments ; and to believe that mission fulfilled, which is but modified and enlarged. This error has led us to break the unity of the conception precisely where it demands the widest extension ; to mistake the function of the eighteenth century, and to make of a negation the point of departure for the nineteenth. We abandoned the religious idea precisely when it was most urgent to revive and extend it until it should embrace the sum of things destined to be transformed, and unite in one grand social conception the forces which are now isolated and divided.

The eighteenth century, too generally regarded as an age of mere scepticism and negation, devoted solely to a labour of criticism, had yet a faith of its own, a mission of its own, and a practical method for the realisation of that mission. Its faith was a Titanic, limitless belief in human power, and in human liberty. Its mission was *to take stock* — if I may be allowed the expression — of the first epoch of the European world ; to sum up, and reduce to a concrete formula, that which eighteen centuries of Christianity had examined, evolved, and achieved ; to constitute the *individual* such as he was destined and designed to be — free, sacred, and inviolable. And this mission it accomplished through the French Revolution — which was the political translation of the Protestant revolution ; a manifestation eminently religious, whatever may be said by those superficial writers who judge a whole period by the errors of individuals, secondary actors in the great drama. The instrument adopted to work out the revolution, and reach the aim it was its mission to achieve, was the idea of *right*. From the theory of *right* it derived its power, its mandate, the legitimacy of its acts. The *declaration of the rights of man* is the supreme and ultimate formula of the French Revolution.

And what, indeed, is man, individual man, if not a right ? In the series of the terms of progress does he not represent the human personality, the element of individual emancipation ? And the aim of the eighteenth century was to fulfil the *human* evolution which had been anticipated and foreseen by the ancients, proclaimed by Christianity, and in part realised by Protestantism. A multitude of obstacles stood between the century and that aim ; every description of impediment and restraint upon the spontaneity and free development of individual faculties ; prohibitions, rules, and precepts limiting human activity ; the tradition of a past activity now decayed ; aristocracies wearing a semblance of intellect and power ; religious forms forbidding movement and advance.

It was necessary to overthrow all these, and the eighteenth century overthrew them. It waged a terrible but victorious war against all things tending to fractionise human power ; to deny movement, or to arrest the flight of intelligence. Every great revolution demands a great idea to be its centre of action ; to furnish it with both lever and fulcrum for the work it has to do. This conception the eighteenth century supplied by placing itself in the centre of its own *subject*. It was the Ego, the human conscience, the *Ego sum* of Christ to the powers of His day.

Firm on that centre as its base, the Revolution, conscious of its own strength and sovereignty by right of conquest, disdained to prove to the world its origin, its link with the past. It simply affirmed. It cried aloud like Fichte : *there is no liberty without equality : all men are equal.* After this it began to deny. It denied the inert past ; it denied feudalism, aristocracy, monarchy. It denied the Catholic * dogma of absolute passivity that poisoned the sources of liberty, and placed despotism at the summit of the social edifice. Ruins there were without end, but in the midst of those ruins and negations one immense affirmation stood erect ; the creature of God, ready to *act*, radiant in power and will ; the *ecce homo*, repeated after eighteen centuries of struggle and suffering ; not by the voice of the martyr, but from the altar raised by the revolution to Victory — Right, the faith of individuality, rooted in the world for ever.

* None can, on any rational grounds, accuse me of failing to recognise the Catholic spirit that presides over the destinies of modern civilisation. All are aware of the meaning generally given to the word *Catholic*. If Catholic had assumed no other meaning than universal, I would call to mind that every religion naturally tends to become Catholic, and most especially so that synthesis which inscribes *Humanity* at the head of its formulæ.

And is this all we seek? Ought man, gifted with progressive activity, to remain quiescent like an emancipated slave, satisfied with his solitary liberty? Does naught remain to him in fulfilment of his mission on earth, but a work of consequences and deductions to be translated into the sphere of fact; or conquests to be watched over and defended?

Because the human *unknown quantity* has been determined, because one among the terms of progress — that of the *individual* — has taken its place among the known and defined quantities, is the series of terms composing the great equation concluded? Is the faculty of progress exhausted? Is naught but rotatory motion left to us?

Because man, consecrated by the power of thought king of the earth, has burst the bonds of a worn-out religious form that imprisoned and restrained his activity and independence, are we to have no new bond of universal fraternity? no religion? no recognised and accepted conception of a general and providential law?

No, eternal God! Thy Word is not all fulfilled; thy thought, the thought of the world, not all revealed. That thought creates still, and will continue to create for ages incalculable by man. The ages that have passed have but revealed to us some fragments of it. Our mission is not concluded. As yet we scarcely know its origin, we

know not its ultimate aim. Time and discovery do
but enlarge its boundaries. It is elevated from age
to age towards destinies unknown to us, seeking the
law of which as yet we know but the first lines.
From initiation to initiation, throughout the series
of thy successive incarnations, this mission has puri-
fied and enlarged the formula of sacrifice ; it learns
the path it has to follow by the study of an eternally
progressive faith. Forms are modified and dis-
solved — religious beliefs are exhausted : the human
spirit leaves them behind as the traveller leaves behind the fires that warmed him through the night,
and seeks another sun. But religion remains : the
idea is immortal, survives the dead forms, and is re-
born from its own ashes. The idea detaches itself
from the worn-out symbol ; disengages itself from
its *involucrum*, which analysis has consumed, and
shines forth in purity and brightness, a new star in
humanity's heaven. How many such shall faith
yet kindle ere the whole path of the future shall be
illumined ? Who shall tell how many stars — secu-
lar thoughts, liberated from every cloud — shall arise
and take their place in the heaven of intellect, ere
man, the living summary of the terrestrial Word,
may declare : *I have faith in myself, my destiny is
accomplished* ?

Such is the law. One labour succeeds another ;
one synthesis succeeds another ; and the latest revealed ever presides over the work we have to ac-

complish, and prescribes its method and organisation. It comprehends all the terms included in the
preceding synthesis, *plus* the new term ; which becomes the *aim* of every endeavour, the unknown
quantity to be determined, and added to the known.
Analysis also has its share in the labour done ; but it
derives its programme and point of departure from
the synthesis of the epoch. Analysis, in fact, has
no life of its own : its existence is merely objective :
it derives its purpose, law, and mission elsewhere.
A portion of every epoch, it is the insignia of none.
Those writers who divide the epochs into two
classes — organic and critical — falsify history. Every epoch is essentially synthetic ; every epoch is
organic. The progressive evolution of the thought
of God, of which our world is the visible manifestation, is unceasingly continuous. The chain cannot
be broken or interrupted. The various *aims* are
united together — the cradle is linked to the tomb.

No sooner, therefore, had the French Revolution concluded one epoch, than the first rays of
another appeared above the horizon. No sooner
had the triumph of the human individual been proclaimed by the charter of rights, than intelligence
foretold a new charter, the charter of *Principles*.
No sooner was the unknown quantity of the so-

called middle ages determined, and the aim of the
Christian synthesis achieved, than a new unknown
quantity, a new aim, was set before the present
generation.

On every side the doubt has arisen — of what
advantage is liberty ? of what advantage equality,
which is in fact but the liberty of all ? What is
the free man but an activity, a force, to be put in
motion ? In what direction shall he move ? As
chance or caprice may direct ? But that is not *life*,
it is a mere succession of acts, of phenomena, of
emissions of vitality, without bond, relation, or con-
tinuity ; it is anarchy. The liberty of the one will
inevitably clash with the liberty of others ; constant strife will arise between individual and individual, and consequent loss of force, and waste of
the productive faculties vouchsafed to us, and which
we are bound to regard as sacred. The liberty of
all, if ungoverned by any general directing law,
will but lead to a state of warfare among men, a
warfare rendered all the more cruel and inexorable
by the virtual equality of the antagonists.

Men deemed they had found a remedy for these
evils when they raised up from the foot of that
cross of Christ which rules above an entire epoch
of the world's history, the formula of fraternity bestowed by the god-like man upon the human race ;
that sublime formula, unknown to the pagan world,

but for which the Christian world had — often unconsciously — fought many a holy fight from the
Crusades to Lepanto. Liberty, equality, and fraternity, inscribed upon every banner, became the
programme of the future, and men attempted to
confine progress within the circle marked out by
those three points. But progress broke through
the circle ; the eternal *cui bono* reappeared. For
we, all of us, demand an *aim*, a human aim. What
is existence other than an aim, and the means of its
achievement ? Now fraternity does not supply
any general social terrestrial aim ; it does not even
imply the necessity of an aim. It has no essential
and inevitable relation with a purpose or intent calculated to harmonise the sum of human faculties and
forces. Fraternity is undoubtedly the basis of all
society, the first condition of social progress, but it
is not progress ; it renders it possible — it is an indispensable element of it — but it is not its definition.
Fraternity is not inconsistent with the theory of
movement in a circle. And the human mind began
to understand these things ; began to perceive that
fraternity, though a necessary link between the
terms liberty and equality — which sum up the individual synthesis — does not pass beyond that synthesis ; that its action is limited to the action of
individual upon individual, that it might be denom-
inated charity, and that though it may constitute a

starting-point whence humanity advances in search of a social synthesis, it may not be substituted for that synthesis.

This being understood, human research recommenced ; men began to perceive that the aim, the function of existence, must also be the ultimate term of that progressive development which constitutes existence itself ; and that, therefore, in order to advance rapidly and directly towards that aim, it was first necessary to determine with exactitude the nature of that progressive development, and to act in accordance with it. *To know the Law, and regulate human activity by the Law :* such is the best mode of stating the problem.

Now the law of the individual can only be deduced from the law of the species. The individual mission can only be ascertained and defined by placing ourselves upon an elevation, enabling us to grasp and comprehend the whole. We must re-ascend to the conception of *Humanity*, in order to ascertain the secret, rule, and law of life of the individual, of man. Hence the necessity of a general co-operation, of harmony of effort, — in a word, of *association* — in order to fulfil the work of all. Hence also the necessity of a complete alteration in the organisation of the revolutionary party, in our theories of government, and in our philosophical, political, and economical studies ; all of which have hitherto been inspired solely by the principle of liberty. The sacred word Humanity, pronounced with a new meaning, has opened up a new world before the eye of genius — a new world as yet only forefelt — and commenced a new epoch.

Is any book required to prove this ? or is a longer explanation and development of the subject necessary in order to prove that such is indeed the actual intellectual movement, and that the labour and business of the age is the discovery of its own synthesis ? Have not all our schools of philosophy for the last twenty years — even when abandoning the true path, and returning to the past — been seeking the great unknown quantity ? Do not even those whose interest it is to lead the human mind away from that search, confess this ? Our Catholicism of the present day seeks to reconcile Gregory VII and Luther ; the Papacy with the freedom and independence of the human spirit. . . And we daily hear the word humanity proffered by the lips of materialists who are incapable of appreciating its meaning, and ever and anon betray their natural tendencies to the individualism of the empire. Whether as a real belief or as an enforced homage, the new epoch obtains its due acknowledgment from intellect almost without exception.

Some of the more fervid apostles of progress lamented a short time ago that our enemies pirated our words without even understanding their meaning. But the complaint is puerile. It is precisely in such agreement, instinctive or compulsory though it be, that we may trace a visible sign of the Word of the new Epoch, Humanity.

Every epoch has a faith of its own. Every synthesis contains the idea of an aim, of a mission. And every mission has its special instrument, its special forces, and its special lever of action. He who should attempt to realise the mission of a given epoch with the instrument of another, would have to pass through an indefinite series of inefficacious endeavours. Overcome by the want of analogy between the means and the end, he might become a martyr, never a victor.

Such is the point to which we have arrived. We all feel, both in heart and brain, the presentiment of a great epoch ; and we have sought to make of the negations and analyses with which the eighteenth century was compelled to surround its newly acquired victory, the banner of the faith of that epoch. Inspired by God to utter the sublime words — regeneration, progress, new mission, the future — we yet persist in striving to realise the material triumph of the programme contained in those words, with the instrument that served for the realisation of a mission now concluded. We invoke a *social* world, a vast harmonious organisation of the forces existing in undirected activity in that vast laboratory, the earth ; — and in order to call this new world into existence, and to lay the foundations of a pacific organisation, we have recourse to those old habits of rebellion which consume our forces within the circle of *individualism*. We proclaim the future from the midst of ruins. Prisoners, whose chain had but been lengthened, we boasted ourselves emancipated and free, because we found ourselves able to move around the column to which we were bound.

It is for this that faith slumbers in the heart of the peoples : for this that the blood of an entire nation fails to rekindle it.

Faith requires an *aim* capable of embracing *life* as a whole, of concentrating all its manifestations, of directing its various modes of activity, or of repressing them all in favour of one alone. It requires an earnest unalterable conviction that that aim will be realised ; a profound belief in a mission, and the obligation to fulfil it ; and the consciousness of a supreme power watching over the path of the faithful towards its accomplishment. These elements are indispensable to faith ; and where any one of these is wanting, we shall have sects, schools, political parties, but no faith ; no constant hourly sacrifice for the sake of a great religious idea.

Now we have no definite religious idea, no profound belief in an obligation entailed by a mission,

no consciousness of a supreme protecting power.
Our actual apostolate is a mere analytical opposition ; our weapons are *interests*, and our chief
instrument of action is a theory of rights. We
are, all of us, notwithstanding our sublime presentiments, the sons of rebellion. We advance, like ren-
egades, without a God, without a law, without a
banner to lead us towards the future. Our former
aim has vanished from our view ; the new, dimly
seen for an instant, is effaced by that doctrine of
rights, which alone directs our labours. We make
of the *individual* both the means and the aim. We
talk of Humanity — a formula essentially religious
— and banish religion from our work. We talk of
synthesis, and yet neglect the most powerful and
active element of human existence. Bold enough
to be undaunted by the dream of the material unity
of Europe, we thoughtlessly destroy its moral unity
by failing to recognise the primary condition of
all association, — uniformity of sanction and belief.
And it is amidst such contradictions that we pre-
tend to renew a world.

I do not exaggerate. I know there are excep-
tions, and I admire them. But the mass of our
party is as I describe it. Its presentiments and desires belong to the new epoch ; the character of its
organisation, and the means of which it seeks to
avail itself, belong to the old. The party has long
had an instinctive sense of a great mission confided

to it ; but it neither understands the true nature of that mission, nor the instruments fitted to achieve it. It is therefore incapable of success, and will remain so until it comprehends that the cry of *"God wills it"* must be the eternal watchword of every undertaking like our own, having sacrifice for its basis, the people for its instrument, and Humanity for its aim.

What ! you complain that faith is dead or dying, that the souls of men are withered by the breath of egotism, and yet you scorn all belief, and proclaim in your writings that religion is no more ; that its day is over, and that there is no religious future for the peoples !

You marvel at the slow advance of the peoples on the path of sacrifice and association, and yet you propose to them a programme of individuality, the sole value of which is negative ; the result of which is a method, not of organisation, but of juxtaposition, which, if analysed, will be found to be nothing more than egotism wrapped in a mantle of philosophic formulæ !

You seek to perform a work of regeneration, and — since without this all political organisation is fruitless — of moral personal amelioration ; and you hope to accomplish it by banishing every religious idea from your work !

Politics merely accept man as he is, in his actual position and character ; define his tendencies, and regulate his action in harmony with them. The religious idea alone has power to transform both.

The religious idea is the very breath of Humanity; its life, soul, conscience, and manifestation. Humanity only exists in the consciousness of its origin and the presentiment of its destiny; and only reveals itself by concentrating its powers upon some one of the intermediate points between these two. Now this is precisely the function of the religious idea. That idea constitutes a faith in an origin common to us all; sets before us, as a principle, a common future; unites all the active faculties in one sole centre, whence they are continuously evolved and developed in the direction of that future, and guides the latent forces of the human mind towards it. It lays hold of life in its every aspect, and in its slightest manifestations; utters its augury over the cradle and the tomb, and affords — philosophically speaking — at once the highest and the most universal formula of a given epoch of civilisation; the most simple and comprehensive expression of its *knowledge* (scientia); the ruling synthesis by which it is governed as a whole, and by which its successive evolutions are directed from on high.

Viewed with regard to the individual, the religious conception is the sign of the relation existing between him and the epoch to which he belongs; the revelation of his function and rule of life; the device beneath which he fulfils it. That conception elevates and purifies the individual, and destroys egotism within him by transporting the centre of activity from the inward to the outward. It has created for man that theory of *duty* which is the parent of sacrifice ; which has inspired, and ever will inspire him to high and holy things ; the sublime theory which brings man nearer to God, lends to the human creature a spark of omnipotence, overleaps every obstacle, and converts the scaffold of the martyr into a ladder of triumph. It is as far above the narrow and imperfect theory of rights, as the law itself is above any one of its consequences.

Right is the faith of the individual. Duty is the common collective faith. Right can but organise resistance : it may destroy, it cannot found. Duty builds up, associates, and unites ; it is derived from a general law, whereas Right is derived only from human will. There is nothing therefore to forbid a struggle against Right : any individual may rebel against any right in another which is injurious to him ; and the sole judge left between the adversaries is Force ; and such, in fact, has frequently been the answer which societies based upon right have given to their opponents.

Societies based upon Duty would not be compelled to have recourse to force ; duty, once admitted as the rule, excludes the possibility of struggle ; and by rendering the individual subject to the general aim, it cuts at the very root of those evils

273754

which Right is unable to prevent, and only affects to cure. Moreover, progress is not a necessary result of the doctrine of Right, it merely admits it as a fact. The exercise of rights being of necessity limited by capacity, progress is abandoned to the arbitrary rule of an unregulated and aimless liberty.

The doctrine of Rights puts an end to sacrifice, and cancels martyrdom from the world : in every theory of individual rights, interests become the governing and motive power, and martyrdom an absurdity, for what interest can endure beyond the tomb ? Yet, how often has martyrdom been the initiation of progress, the baptism of a world !

Every doctrine not based upon Progress considered as a necessary law, is inferior to the idea and the demands of the epoch. Yet the doctrine of rights still rules us with sovereign sway ; rules even that republican party which assumes to be the party of progress and initiation in Europe ; and the liberty of the republicans — although they instinctively proffer the words duty, sacrifice, and mission — is still a theory of resistance ; their religion — if indeed they speak of any — a formula of the relation between God and the individual ; the political organisation they invoke and dignify by the name of *social*, a mere series of defences raised up around laws framed to secure the liberty of *each* to follow out his *own* aim, his own tendencies, and his own interests ; their definition of the Law does not

go beyond the expression of the general will ; their
formula of association is society founded on Rights ;
their faith does not overpass the limits traced out
nearly a century ago by a man — himself the incarnation of struggle — in a declaration of rights.
Their theories of government are theories of
distrust ; their organic problem, a remnant of
patched-up Constitutionalism, reduces itself to the
discovery of a point around which individuality
and association, liberty and law, may oscillate for
ever in resultless hostility ; their *people* is too often
a *caste* — the most useful and numerous it is true —
in open rebellion against other castes, and seeking to
enjoy in its turn the rights given by God to all ;
their republic is the turbulent intolerant democracy
of Athens ; * their war-cry a cry of vengeance, and
their symbol Spartacus.

Now this is the eighteenth century over again
— its philosophy ; its *human* synthesis ; its mate-

* The word democracy, although it expresses energetically and
with historical precision the secret of the ancient world, is — like
all the political phrases of antiquity — below the conception of
the future Epoch which we republicans are bound to initiate.
The expression *Social Government* would be preferable as in-
dicative of the idea of association, which is the life of the Epoch.
The word democracy was inspired by an idea of rebellion, sacred
at the time, but still rebellion. Now every such idea is imperfect, and inferior to the idea of unity which will be the dogma
of the future. Democracy is suggestive of struggle ; it is the
cry of Spartacus, the expression and manifestation of a people
in its first arising. Government — the social institution — repre-
sents a people triumphant ; a people that constitutes itself. The
gradual extinction of aristocracy will cancel the word democracy.

rialist policy ; its spirit of analysis and Protestant criticism ; its sovereignty of the individual ; its negation of an ancient religious formula ; its distrust of all authority ; its spirit of emancipation and resistance. It is the French Revolution over again ; the past, with the addition of a few presentiments ; servitude to old things surrounded with a prestige of youth and novelty.

The past is fatal to our party. The French Revolution — I say it with deep conviction — crushes us. It weighs like an incubus upon our hearts, and forbids them to beat. Dazzled by the grandeur of that titanic struggle, we prostrate ourselves before it even yet. We expect its programme to furnish us with both men and things ; we strive to copy Robespierre and St. Just, and search the records of the *Clubs* of 1791 and 1793 for titles to give to the *sections* of 1833 and 1834. But while we thus ape our fathers, we forget that their greatness consisted in the fact that they aped no one. They derived their inspiration from contemporary sources, from the wants of the masses, from the elements by which they were surrounded. And it was precisely because the instruments they used were adapted to the aim they had in view, that they achieved miracles.

Why should we not do as they have done?
Why, while we study and respect tradition, should
we not advance? It is our duty to venerate our
fathers' greatness, and to demand of their sepulchres
a pledge of the future, but not the future itself;
God alone, the Father of all revelations and of all
epochs, can direct us upon its boundless path.

Let us arise, therefore, and endeavour to be great
in our turn. To be so, we must comprehend our
mission in all its completeness. We — the men of
the present — are standing between two epochs;
between the tomb of one world and the cradle of
another; between the boundary-line of the individual synthesis and the confines of the synthesis Humanity. What we have to do is to fix our eyes
upon the future while we break the last links of the
chain that binds us to the past, and deliberately advance. We have emancipated ourselves from the
abuses of the past; let us now emancipate ourselves
from its glories. The eighteenth century has done
its work. Our fathers sleep proudly and calmly in
their tombs: they repose, wrapped in their flag, like
warriors after a battle. Fear not to offend them.
Their banner, dyed red in the blood of Christ,
transmitted by Luther to the *Convention*, to be
raised upon the corpses of those slain in the battles
of the peoples, is a sacred legacy to us all. None
will venture to lay hands upon it; and we will return hereafter and lay at its foot, where our fathers

lie buried, the laurels we have won in our turn.

Our present duty is to found the policy of the nineteenth century ; to re-ascend, through philosophy, to faith ; to define and organise association ; to proclaim Humanity ; to initiate a new epoch. Upon that initiation does the material realisation of the past epoch depend.

These things are not new. I know it, and confess it gladly. My voice is but one among many that have announced nearly the same ideas ; affirming that *association* is the fundamental principle by which our political labours should henceforth be directed. Many great men have condemned the exclusive worship of the doctrine of Rights, the ultimate formula of *individuality* now degenerating into materialism : many schools, both past and present, have invoked Duty, as the anchor of salvation for society tormented by inefficacious aspirations.

Why then do I insist so much upon their want of foresight ? What matters it whether they preach the adoption of this term as the centre of a new programme, or only as a development of the old ? So long as they join with us in crying *forward !* what matters it that they persist in confounding *association* with *fraternity* ; or Humanity — the complex unity of all the human faculties organised in the pursuit of the same aim — with the liberty and equality of all men ? Wherefore, by promulgating the idea of a new epoch, create a new enterprise and consequently new difficulties?

Is our question then a mere question of words alone ?

I do not think so.

It is important to affirm the new epoch : to affirm that what we now preach is in fact a new programme ; and this for a reason that should be universally recognised and admitted. We desire not merely to think, but to act. We are seeking not merely the emancipation of a people, and of some other peoples through it, but the emancipation of the peoples.

Now the true emancipation of the peoples can only be effected through the conscience of the peoples. They will not act efficaciously until they recognise a newly revealed *aim*, for the realisation of which the labour of all, the equality of all, and an *initiative*, are required. Until they arrive at the recognition of such an aim, there is no hope of faith, sacrifice, or active enthusiasm from them. They will remain inert ; and, dominated by the prestige of the previous initiative, they will leave the duty of realising and exhausting its consequences to that people who by assuming the glory of the initiative rendered themselves responsible for its fulfilment.

They will be content to follow slowly in their footsteps, but do no more. And if, for reasons to them unknown, that people should stop short upon the way, they will stop short also. Silence, inaction, and suspension of life will follow. Such is the spectacle presented by Europe at the present day.

The idea of a new epoch, by implying a new aim to be reached, leaves the initiative to the future, and thereby awakens the general conscience to activity. It substitutes spontaneity for imitation ; the achievement of a special mission for the mere performance of an executive part in the mission of others ; Europe for France. We thus furnish a new element of revolutionary activity.

By the affirmation of a new epoch, we affirm the existence of a new synthesis ; a general idea destined to embrace all the terms of the anterior synthesis, *plus* one ; and starting from that new term to co-ordinate all the historical series, all the facts, all the manifestations of life, all the aspects of the human problem, all the branches of human knowledge that are ranged beneath it. We give a new and fruitful impulse to the labours of intelligence ; we proclaim the necessity of a new encyclopædia, which, by summing up and comprehending all the progress achieved, would constitute a new progress in itself. We place beyond all controversy, in the rank of ascertained truths, all the terms which have been the aim of past revolutions, — the liberty, equality, and fraternity of men, and of peoples.

We separate ourselves for ever from the epoch of exclusive individuality, and, still more decisively therefore, from that individualism which is the materialism of that epoch. We close up the paths to the past.

And finally, by that affirmation we reject every doctrine of eclecticism and transition; every imperfect formula containing the statement of a problem without any attempt to solve it; every school seeking to conjoin life and death, and to renew the world through the medium of an extinct synthesis.

By the very character of the epoch we proclaim, we furnish a new basis to the principle of universal suffrage; we elevate the political question to the height of a philosophical conception; we constitute an apostolate of Humanity by asserting that common law of nations which should be the sign of our faith. We consecrate those sudden spontaneous collective movements of the people which will initiate and translate the new synthesis in action. We lay the foundations of an humanitarian faith, to the height of which the republican party must elevate itself in order to succeed. For every epoch has its baptism of faith: our epoch lacks that baptism as yet, but we can at least make ourselves its precursors.

VI

ON CÆSARISM

Anyone familiar with any part of my writings will surely not accuse me of irreverence toward genius, or of sharing in an anarchical tendency that is so conspicuous today, and which thwarts many a noble endeavour by inclining insignificant individuals to hold aloof, under pretext of personal independence, from any activity that implies orderliness, subordination and discipline. I respect authority and I am conscious of all the holiness that lies in obedience to a leader. However, authority resides in God, in His law, in the truth. When, therefore, a man bids me to follow him and says, "Authority lives in my person," I have the duty and the right to investigate and see whether virtue, the moral law, the capacity for self-sacrifice are in fact alive in his person, just whither he intends to lead me, and whether, finally, the sum of forces that he is in a position to apply to the achievement of the given purpose is larger or smaller than the resources possessed by some other individual. If those three researches turn out in his favour, I am ready to follow him in reverent and joyous trust, without holding the motives of his every act in suspicion, without requiring an explanation for his every gesture, without tormenting him with distracting queries or unworthy doubts.

The theory that is expounded in this book * suppresses two terms of the above statement of the problem and holds that the third is alone sufficient to legitimise authority. We should fall on our faces before authority, much as savages prostrate themselves before the flash of lightning, whenever, wherever, and whithersoever authority announces itself. Attila would kill the conscience of the human race !

As a matter of fact, genius is nothing more than a resource, an instrument. It may be applied to evil. It may wallow in selfishness. It may promote the progress of all. Genius is not authority. It is the tool of authority. Authority is virtue illumined by genius. Genius increases duties and responsibilities. Duty is always something proportionate to the power or opportunity that an individual or a group of individuals has. Genius by itself does not constitute title to sovereignty. The purpose alone is sovereign. Anyone who loses track of these criteria of judgment is destined forever to misunderstand the history of men and of the world.

It is not true that genius is always and by nature the motive force of new eras. Genius now initiates, now interprets, now epitomises, now closes eras. At times, toward the end of an era, when the idea that has inspired it is exhausted, in the intellectual

* *Jules César*, published anonymously by Louis Napoleon Bonaparte.

field at least, when the human spirit, under the drive of an inexorable law of progress, is beginning to hope and to seek for a new source of inspiration, some genius will suddenly appear and take his stand on the untrodden ground of the future — beyond the limits, that is, of the tradition that has hitherto prevailed. His soul will be seen to flame with boundless aspiration just as his brow is radiant with the glow of a new dawn. Holy through unconscious virtue and brotherly love, he will seem instinctively to formulate the synthesis of the future as he states its guiding ideal in words. Thereafter, ten, twelve, a score of centuries will talk of him.

Then again, at such times, in the period, that is, between a dying epoch and the new age that is coming on, another sort of man will appear, a man whose talent lies in capacities for action and for ruling others. He will summarise all that has gone before in his person, realise it in institutions, spread it, in its characteristic traits, over lands different from the ones in which it found its visible and triumphant expression. Such a man unwittingly prepares the ground for the idea of the future. He does not reveal it. He does not even know or understand it.

The man of the first type is an initiator. He is a prophet. The man of the second type is a summariser. He epitomises the thought of an era and spreads it abroad. He creates nothing new. There is so little of the creator in him that, as a rule, he takes with him to the tomb all the creative energy of the people from whom he derived his power and his glory. The mission that Greece had in the world perished for indefinitely long ages with Alexander. The lingering death agony of Rome began with Julius Cæsar. The leadership of France in Europe ended with Napoleon.

Religious geniuses belong to the first category. Almost all conquerors belong to the second. The religious prophet generally meets the conditions of authority that I have specified above. He has a programme. His life is consistent with his preaching. He gives a pledge of moral potency through the spell he exercises over human souls. The conqueror, on the other hand, the only genius envisaged by the system that I am combatting under the name of Cæsarism, replaces the requirements mentioned with an energetic, over-bearing, assertion of self. To anyone who asks: "Why should I believe in you?" he invariably answers: "Because I believe in myself." Such a man can do startling things, but he cannot open an era. Initiative of that sort implies apostleship, armed or pacific, of a new ideal. If the conqueror had one, he would offer it as a bond for the trust he exacts.

Now people can serve ideas. People cannot, without playing false to their mission on earth, serve mere individuals. We can follow them as long as an ideal, which we are free to ponder by ourselves and accept if we choose, can be seen resplendent on the flags they wave. When there is no such flag, when there is no idea that gives bond for the leader's intentions, incumbent upon us is the duty of examining each and every act of the man who bids us to follow him. It is our duty to preserve our freedom intact, as the guarantor and the instrument of our examination. It is our duty to protest with word and sword against every effort that is made to deprive us of that freedom. I believe in God and I worship His law. I abhor idolatry.

A deep and persistent confusing of two essentially different things lies at the bottom of Cæsarism. The agent is inevitably confused with the objective results of his career, even the remote and incidental results. The instrument is confused with the law that should control the agent's action. The man is mistaken for God. World history slowly evolves from the continuous interplay of two forces : the activity of individuals and the design of Providence. The word that defines the first is liberty. The word that defines the second is progress. Time and space are ours. We can retard or accelerate progress. We cannot prevent it.

Progress is the law of God. That law will be carried out, whatever we do. But its progressive fulfilment does not relieve us of responsibility for our acts or even reduce the amount of our responsibility. The sins and mistakes of one generation serve as lessons to succeeding generations; but the generation that sins or errs deserves blame or punishment, and punishment it will suffer, either here on earth or elsewhere.

The invasions of the Latin world by the races of the North destroyed Roman civilization. They gave Italy over to massacres and plunderings of every description and established conditions of semi-barbarism on lands that had once known free citizenship, art and industry. Some centuries later we find the Roman world replaced by a Latin-German world. Civilization had recovered in extension what it had lost in depth and intensity. The barbarians had carried back to their forests many influences from the civilisation with which they had been at mortal grips. So a vast field had been opened and prepared for a new synthesis, in other words, for Christian civilisation. Well, in view of that, are we to admire Alaric and Attila as standard-bearers of civilisation? Should the sons of Romans have enrolled under the banners of the invaders?

During the later Middle Ages men who spilled oceans of blood to vent their thirst for dominion founded monarchies, and so unwittingly prepared the ground for our modern nationalities, which in turn today are summoning the peoples to a consciousness of their collective existence and so are preparing the ground for the destruction of monarchical dogma and for the triumph of republicanism. Should we on that account glorify and venerate the treachery and the cruelty of a Louis XI or others like him ?

Every tyranny, even the worst sort of tyranny, leads infallibly in ten, twenty, thirty years, to a greater development of freedom. By a law that seems to be basic in the nature of things, the human spirit proportions its activity to the pressure that is exerted upon it. Are we therefore bound to raise altars to our tyrants ? There was an ancient heresy that worshipped Judas ; for, so it was argued, had it not been for Judas there would have been no crucifixion and therefore no redemption. Cæsarism is an application to history of just such a heresy. No ! We cannot confuse the acts of the free responsible creature with the objective workings of providential laws. Curses upon Judas, and glory be to God, who allows no Judas to change humanity's destinies ! That we raise that twin war cry is a vital condition to human living, if the achievement of those destinies is not to be too long postponed.

VII

AGAINST DICTATORSHIP

In 1833, on publishing an article by Buonarroti, *Upon the Government of a People during the period of Insurrection for Liberty*, signed Camillo, in a number of Young Italy, I protested against a paragraph advocating an individual dictatorship, in the following note :

"We agree with all the views put forth in this article, except that which admits of individual dictatorship, among the forms of revolutionary government.

"We dissent from this view, because, although the nature of the governing power required during the period of insurrection is essentially different from the form of government to be adopted after victory, there are two conditions which it is absolutely requisite that it should fulfil. The first is that it should avoid all resemblance to the nature of the power overthrown ; the second, that it should contain the germ at least of the form of government intended to be substituted for that power. Both of these conditions exclude the dominion of one man, and indicate the dominion of the majority.

"Because, although the revolutionary power ought to be composed of the most virtuous and gifted in heart and intellect, and it is unadvisable to summon parliaments or numerous assemblies in moments where the governmental acts and decrees are required to succeed one another with the rapidity of military movements ; we believe, nevertheless, that the governing power should contain one representative of every insurgent province of Italy.

"Because the dictatorship of a single individual may become dangerous in the highest degree among a people accustomed to the degrading influences of servitude.

"Because, until the day arrive when a truly national government, the issue of free and universal suffrage, shall be formed, an element of distrust will always exist among a people striving for emancipation ; and the concentration of all the revolutionary forces in the hands of one man would render every description of guarantee illusory.

"Because, in Italy, as in all enslaved countries, there exist no elements by which to judge and select the man possessed of sufficient virtue, energy, constancy, and knowledge of men and things, to enable him worthily to govern and direct the destiny of twenty-six millions of men. He could only be proved worthy by the experience of many years of vicissitude, during which he had passed uncontaminated through those trials and situations most calculated to corrupt ; and during that period of trial the insurrection would require a government and an administration.

"Should the idea of an individual dictatorship be generally accepted, it might place the supreme power, perhaps a crown, at the disposal of the first soldier favoured by fortune in battle."

VIII

YOUNG EUROPE

General Instructions for the Initiators

1

Young Europe is an association of men believing in a future of liberty, equality, and fraternity, for all mankind ; and desirous of consecrating their thoughts and actions to the realisation of that future.

General Principles

2

One sole God ; One sole ruler, — His Law ; One sole interpreter of that law, — Humanity.

3

To constitute humanity in such wise as to enable it throughout a continuous progress to discover and apply the law of God by which it should be governed, as speedily as possible : such is the mission of *Young Europe.*

4

As our true well-being consists in living in accordance with the law of our being, the knowledge and fulfilment of the law of humanity is the sole source of good. The fulfilment of the mission of *Young Europe* will result in the general good.

5

Every mission constitutes a pledge of duty.

Every man is bound to consecrate his every faculty to its fulfilment. He will derive his rule of action from the profound conviction of that duty.

6

Humanity can only arrive at the knowledge of its Law of Life, through the free and harmonious development of all its faculties.

Humanity can only reduce that knowledge to action through the free and harmonious development of all its faculties.

Association is the sole means of realising this development.

7

No true association is possible save among free men and equals.

8

By the law of God, given by Him to humanity, all men are free, are brothers, and are equals.

9

Liberty is the right of every man to exercise his faculties without impediment or restraint, in the accomplishment of his special mission, and in the choice of the means most conducive to its accomplishment.

10

The free exercise of the faculties of the individual, may in no case violate the rights of others. The special mission of each man must be accomplished in harmony with the general mission of Humanity. There is no other limit to human liberty.

11

Equality implies the recognition of uniform rights and duties for all men — for none may escape the action of the law by which they are defined — and every man should participate, in proportion to his labour, in the enjoyment of the produce resulting from the activity of all the social forces.

12

Fraternity is the reciprocal affection, the sentiment which inclines man to do unto others as he would that others should do unto him.

13

All privilege is a violation of equality.

All arbitrary rule is a violation of Liberty.

Every act of egotism is a violation of Fraternity.

14

Wheresoever privilege, arbitrary rule, or egotism are introduced into the social constitution, it is the duty of every man who comprehends his own mission to combat them by every means in his power.

15

That which is true of each individual with regard to the other individuals forming a part of the society to which he belongs, is equally true of every people with regard to humanity.

16

By the law of God, given by God to humanity, all the peoples are free — are brothers and are equals.

17

Every people has its special mission, which will co-operate towards the fulfilment of the general mission of humanity. That mission constitutes its *nationality*. Nationality is sacred.

18

All unjust rule, all violence, every act of egotism exercised to the injury of a people, is a violation of

the liberty, equality, and fraternity of the peoples.
All the peoples should aid and assist each other in
putting an end to it.

19

Humanity will only be truly constituted when all
the peoples of which it is composed have acquired
the free exercise of their sovereignty, and shall be
associated in a Republican Confederation, governed
and directed by a common Declaration of Principles
and a common Pact, towards the common aim —
the discovery and fulfilment of the Universal Moral
Law.

These two acts were signed for the Italians by
L. A. Melagari, Giacomo Ciani, Gaspare Rosales,
Ruffini, Ghiglioni, and myself : others signed for the
Poles and Germans.   Afterwards our little group
separated and dispersed in different cantons.

The ideal of the association of *Young Europe* was
the federal organisation of European democracy under one sole direction ; so that any nation arising in
insurrection should at once find the others ready to
assist it — if not by action, at least by a moral support sufficiently powerful to prevent hostile intervention on the part of their governments.   We
therefore decided to constitute a National Committee of each nation, around which all the elements of
republican progress might rally by degrees, and ar-

ranged that all these committees should be linked with our Central Provisional Committee of the Association, through the medium of a regular correspondence.

We diffused secret rules for the affiliation of members, decided upon the formula of oath to be taken, and chose — as the common symbol — an ivy leaf. In short, we took all the measures necessary for the formation of a secret association. I did not deceive myself, however, by an exaggerated conception of the extent or diffusion of the association, nor imagine it possible that it should ever attain any compact force capable of being brought into action. I knew that it embraced too vast a sphere to allow of any practical results, and that much time and many severe lessons would be required in order to teach the peoples the necessity of a true European fraternity. My only aim, therefore, was to constitute an apostolate of *ideas* different from those then current, and to leave them to bear fruit how and where they might.

IX

REPLY TO THE GERMAN NATIONALISTS

Yes, I have ambitions for my country, once it has become a country, and I am willing to state them, not so much to you as to Germany as a whole, a country that has our affection and esteem and by which we of the Italian Nationalist Party are concerned to be understood. I want my country to take the lead in the betterment of all countries and in a transformation of Europe. I want my country to furnish the moral impulse for a condition of things that will be different from the systematised anarchy in which, like galvanised corpses, we are floundering about today ; for a condition of things that will protect and establish the life of God wherever the latter bursts forth in spontaneous manifestations ; that will divide Europe into great and united nations according to natural affinities ; that will hereafter prevent dynastic ambitions from driving the peoples into patricidal wars ; that will save us Italians from the temptation of following the deceptive lead of Louis Napoleon, and you Germans from the temptation of becoming the prop of evil — I mean of the House of Hapsburg. You Germans proclaim the holy inviolability of thought. Is it worthy of you, therefore, to be afraid of any sincere aspiration however powerful ? Would you really strangle Italy's national life in its infancy in dread lest some day we shall attain an inordinate expansion ?

I look back over the history of my country and I find that whenever Italy has lived a life of her own with a thought of her own, her life has been the life of all and her thought the thought of a united humanity. Before me, in the pages of history, stand the Capitol and the Vatican. I see the Rome of the

Cæsars (or rather the Rome of the Republic, for the Cæsars did what Louis Napoleon is doing today : They replaced the thought of all with the thought of themselves, thereby introducing a deadly germ of decadence into the civilising mission of Rome). And I see the Rome of the Popes. Is it any fault of mine if I catch the vision of a greater mission for a third Rome, the Rome of the Italian people ? Since 1815 no one has been taking the initiative for progress in Europe. Is it a crime for me to call out to my country — "Seize that initiative ! Take that lead !" ?

I look out over the present and what do I find ? I find that among all nationalities we Italians alone have the double obstacle — perhaps I should call it the twin privilege — of the Hapsburg Empire and the Papacy. Is it any fault of mine that we can become a nation only on condition that, first, nationality, in other words, liberty for the peoples, and second, freedom of conscience, proclaimed for all lands in the world that are without it, shall follow as inexorable consequences from the bald fact of Italy's existence ?

Do as I do ! Dream as I dream ! You came of yore into our lands to protest in the name of human liberty against the material absorption with which the Cæsars were supplanting Italy's civilising thought. Centuries later, with the applause of half the world, you raised another protest through the ringing voice of Luther. Consider those two

mighty manifestations of German nationality and
find in them the duty to say a third great thing :
"That conquest by might does not make right — nor
treaties either, when they are made in the interests
of a few individuals called kings ! Humanity knows
only one principle of right : the good and the just."

You accuse me of claiming leadership for my
country. Take the lead yourselves ! You will win
our wholehearted applause. We will follow you
down the fair road. We will achieve great things
together. Emulation is the secret of greatness among
the peoples.

But in the name of all that is sacred in our ideal, in
the name of all that is productive and truly religious
in the future we hold before our eyes, do not reduce
the great question that is being debated in Europe
today to a question of determining just how many
slaves will pass from the uniform of one master to
the uniform of another on this or that area of soil.
Do not justify oppression by making the peoples its
sponsors. You are men of thought, men of progress.
Do not shoulder arms for Foreign Offices that date
from the Middle Ages ! "Be Germans !" is what
you say to your people. In what sense do you use
that expression ? Of what Germany are you thinking ? Of the Germany that oppresses in the name
of violence, or of the Germany that blesses in the
name of science and civilisation ? Of the Germany
of Luther, or of the Germany of Metternich ? I am

a foreigner but I know a Germany before which I always bow, hat in hand. It is the Germany of the Reformation that said to the world : "Freedom of conscience." It is the Germany that at that time spoke through her greatly underestimated peasantry and said : "The Kingdom of Heaven must have some counterpart on earth." It is the Germany that later spoke through the glorious line of her philosophers from Lessing to Bauer and said : "Ponder earnestly these three great things : Thought, History, Religion !"

But to fulfil her mission in the world this Germany does not need the triangle between Trent, Roveredo and the Adige ! What she needs is unity. What she needs is consistency between thought and action so that no one can say : "She is preaching to-day what tomorrow she will repudiate in conduct." She needs to cleanse herself of the crimes of her dynasties, throw off the burden of injustices that Austria has seen fit to load upon her. She needs love and respect from the peoples, not suspicion and warfare. She needs to gather her own human resources together and use them to her utmost advantage on the soil where her language is spoken and where mothers at the cradles of their little ones recite the legends of her people. She must not waste her men by camping them in places where they can remain only as hostile legions facing hostile legions. Such the Germany that I am addressing in these times. Now this Germany cannot achieve her unity till the Hapsburg Empire has fallen. This Germany will not win the love of the peoples, she will not be able to marshal her human resources, she will not attain to consciousness of her mission, so long as her sons are sent to fight side by side with the Croats — whom you also, gentlemen, seem not to love — against the national independence of people who have done them no wrong, who can never become dangerous to them, but who do ask to be masters of their own destinies.

You argue from a theory of interest, I from a theory of principles, for without principles no abiding interests are possible. You are evidently not Germans, save in a purely material, purely local sense of the term. I am an Italian, but at the same time I am a European. I love my country because I love the concept of country. I believe in freedom for Italians because I believe in the concept of freedom. I want rights for Italians, because I believe in rights for all. Nationality is a holy thing in my eyes. In it I see an instrument for labor toward the common good, toward progress for all. Geographical situation, historical traditions, language, special aptitudes, are in my eyes outward indications of nationality ; but the mission that a nationality fulfils, or is called to fulfil, is its baptism and its birthright. The nation must stand toward all humanity as the family stands, or ought to stand, toward country. If a nation works for the wrong, if it oppresses others, if it comes out as a missionary of injustice in behalf of a temporary interest, it loses its right to exist as a nation — it digs its own grave. That is all there is to my "disingenuous" doctrine of nationality.

I should be renouncing my good Italian faith if I could ever bring myself to say to Italy : "Make provision against a possible attack from Germany by fortifying yourself on the Drava-Sava line." I should consider myself a traitor to my country were I ever to say : "Germany is a menace. We must weaken the enemy wherever we can. Join hands with Louis Napoleon, therefore, on the day of his inevitable advance upon the Rhine."

You think that you can stand above these humble norms of political morality. You are saying to Germany : "Venice is not yours. By race, language, geography, associations, and finally by desire of her own inhabitants, Venice is Italian. Austrian rule hangs on in Venice only in virtue of the bayonet and the hangman. Nevertheless, the exercise of a right which you are asked to recognise may someday be dangerous to you. Deny it therefore ! Uphold tyranny ! Stamp on freedom !" But I say to you : Your best assurance against the possibility of danger from Italy lies in the love and alliance of a grateful Italian people. You prefer to trust to the guns of the Quadrilateral. Evidently, then, there is no basis for an understanding between us. Between your outlook and mine yawns the gulf that separates right from might, eternal law from the manœuvre of the moment, oppression from freedom.

You imagine that in that way you are helping your German fatherland. No one can ever do good to a country, gentlemen, by asking it to dishonor itself. There is a law of retribution in the world, a law stronger than all the sophistries of a materialistic selfishness, a law stronger than the strongest fortress that it is possible for man to build. That laws reads : "Injustice shall not prevail for ever. Oppression is suicide." You can trace the workings of that law through the whole course of history. It can be seen working in our time in the present situation of Austria, in the uncontrollable process of disintegration that is going on within her empire, in that cry of nationality which she thought she had drowned in sophistries and in the blood of the martyrs but which, whether one like it nor not, is today rising anew and in unison from the innermost hearts of ten different peoples.

Listen, gentlemen : You are not going to keep Venice for Austria. As surely as I sit here writing these words, Venice is going to be Italian, and before very long. There is no human force great enough to prevent that. If my only thought, therefore, were of Italy, I might well be silent, leaving my answer to the course of events.

But suppose Germany were to heed you ! What

would the consequences of your wretched policy be ? The dangers that would be threatening you — not from the Alps but on the Rhine — would be no whit diminished. They would simply be increased by the anger of a people that has suddenly come to life with all its courage and noble instincts but is uncertain as to the road before it and is eager, therefore, for external support. Your cause would be isolated in Europe ; and you would have done nothing but strengthen the one power of which you really need be afraid, the prestige, against which we are all campaigning, of a flag that enjoys the popular sympathies of Europe.

For thirty years I have been fighting, within the limits of my poor resources, any authority that fails to represent justice, truth, progress and fails to recognise the consent of the peoples as the seal of right. That authority I have fought under whatever name it chanced to bear — Czar, Pope, Bonaparte, oppressor nation. In spite of the years that have passed my soul is still young. It rears and thrills at the inspiring rise of any people that has caught the vision of a new age and a new life. But I fall back into sorrow and doubt as I see the support that is being given, blindly, irresponsibly, to the one power in Europe that is postponing the dawn of the new age and strangling, or at least distorting, the new life.

Today in Europe there is only one real danger. It is not the danger that Venice shall be free ; or that a half million Italians living in the Tyrol or on the southern slopes of the Alps shall be united to their mother country ; or that the weakling House of Savoy shall for a time garner the harvest of the revolutionary movement. The danger is imperialism. The danger is that the Czar of the West may succeed in wrapping the usurper ambitions of the Bonapartes in the folds of a flag that Europe reveres as the flag of regeneration and justice. The danger is that thirty-seven million Frenchmen, valiant, strong in a powerful sense of country, enamoured of glory, shall grow accustomed to viewing that man as the incarnation of a great idea.

And it is painful to me to see how the very men who loathe and dread that power are unwittingly playing its game and furthering its designs. Louis Napoleon has something that the men who are ruling England, and that you, too, gentlemen, do not have : He has the wit to see that the principle of nationality is omnipotent and that the hour for reorganising Europe in the light of that principle is at hand. His idea is that, since the principle of nationality cannot be suppressed, it is the wiser part to monopolise it, divert it from the channels it would naturally follow, strip it of everything that is hostile to absolutism, limit it, adulterate its character, replace the question of freedom with the territorial question, make it an instrument of power for selfish ends, for the progressive expansion of his own family line and of imperial France. In that lies the whole secret of Louis Napoleon's might.

Now what was required for meeting a manœuvre of that character ? One had only to understand what he understood, to adopt, with nobler intent, the policy that he adopted. If, in 1857, England had replied favorably to the advances made by Piedmont, if, courageously drawing the consequences of the language that was used at the Paris conferences, she had come out openly in support of the Italian cause, Louis Napoleon would not have been in a position to pose as the sole patron of a free and united Italy, and there would have been no Peace of Villafranca, no cession of Savoy and Nice.

If, today, Germany were to meet Austria with a public opinion unanimously favorable to justice, if she were openly to dissociate herself from the cause of the oppressors in Venetia, if, in concert with England, she were rigorously to apply the principle of non-intervention in Italy and insist on the immediate recall of the French troops in Rome, she would be rewarded with the enthusiastic friendship of Italy ; she would free us from subjection to imperial France, weaken the only enemy of whom she need be afraid, establish a precedent against any foreign intervention in German affairs, remove pretexts for the attack that is now in view on the Rhine, and make impossible the help in that enterprise which Louis Bonaparte is asking of Italy and which Cavour, as the price to be paid for Rome, is thinking of giving him.

By following a consistently negative policy, by withholding any open and direct support from Italy, by extending — What inconceivable ingenuousness ! — every assurance to imperial France as to her resolve not to intervene, England has driven Italy into the arms of Louis Napoleon, made Louis Napoleon the arbiter of Continental policy, and today offers the dispiriting spectacle of a country that foresees war in a near future, is arming for that war, and is meantime leaving to the enemy free choice of moment and terrain and perfect freedom to occupy all the important positions that will facilitate his victory.

Now you, gentlemen, are stepping forward as defenders of a power which, for you, as for us, is the representative of evil. You are threatening to join Austria in order to prevent us from obtaining what is ours. Instead of taking up the flag of nationality and calling it your own in the name of freedom, you are vainly denying the principle of nationality, which is certain to triumph. If Germany were to follow your advice you would be postponing the achievement of your national unity indefinitely ; you would be besmirching the brow of your country with an undying shame ; you would be offering Louis Napoleon a pretext he is looking for and a slogan that would win him the sympathy of the peoples ; you would be forcing the Italian Foreign Office to support the Bonapartist policy which we are fighting, and which we urge you to fight as our comrades.

Germany can be saved from the dangers that threaten her not by fighting along the line of the Mincio, but by founding German national unity, by facilitating the unification of an independent Italy, by helping Hungary and Poland to become free nations. In that way only can the Czar of the West and the Czar of the North be dealt with at the same time.

I have considered it important to repeat these things to Germany in the interests of the common cause, and I thank you, gentlemen, for the opportunity you have given me for doing so. A crisis in Europe is at hand. Of it will come either slavery or freedom for the world for several generations. Every people, every individual, has the right and the duty to cry aloud to his brethren : "Beware ! The time has come to choose, logically, courageously, between good and evil, between justice and injustice, between freedom for the peoples and Russian, French, Austrian imperialism. Those who persist in wavering between the two alternatives will be crushed between them."

As for you, gentlemen, may I give you one word of counsel. When one enters upon a discussion in a sincere quest for the truth and with a man who has aged in the struggle for the sacredness of conscience and for what, rightly or mistakenly, he judges to be the truth, any insinuations as to "secret designs," pretences, "demagogic trickeries" are not only in bad taste but are also tainted with an unfairness that is dishonouring to those who resort to them. Try to abstain from such things hereafter. From such an unchivalrous choice of weapons one might argue that your hearts are not as persuaded as they might be of the righteousness of your cause.

X

TEMPEST OF DOUBTS

The last months of that year had inured me to suffering, and rendered me

> "On all sides
> Well squared to fortune's blows"

as Dante has it. I know not to what peculiarity of mind it is owing that I have never been able to remember the dates of even the most important events of my individual life. But were I to live for a century I could never forget the close of that year, nor the moral tempest that passed over me, and amid the vortex of which my soul was so nearly overwhelmed. I speak of it now with reluctance, and solely for the sake of those who may be doomed to suffer what I then suffered, and to whom the voice of a brother who has escaped from that tempest — storm-beaten and bleeding indeed, but with retempered soul — may perhaps indicate the path of salvation.

It was the tempest of Doubt, which I believe all who devote their lives to a great enterprise, yet have not dried and withered up their soul — like Robespierre — beneath some barren intellectual formula, but have retained a loving heart, are doomed — once at least — to battle through. My soul was overflowing with and greedy of affection ; as fresh and eager to unfold to joy as in the days when sustained by my mother's smile ; as full of fervid hope, for others at least, if not for myself. But during those fatal months there darkened around me such hurricane of sorrow, disillusion, and deception, as to bring before my eyes, in all its ghastly nakedness, a foreshadowing of the old age of my soul, solitary, in a desert world, wherein no comfort in the struggle was vouchsafed to me.

It was not only the overthrow, for an indefinite period, of every Italian hope ; the dispersion of the best of our party ; the series of persecutions, which had undone the work we had done in Switzerland, and driven us away from the spot nearest Italy ; the exhaustion of our means, and the accumulation of almost insurmountable material obstacles between me and the task I had set myself to do ; — it was the falling to pieces of that moral edifice of faith and love from which alone I had derived strength for the combat ; — the scepticism I saw rising around me upon every side ; — the failure of faith in those who had solemnly bound themselves with me to pursue unshaken the path we had known at the outset to be choked with sorrows ; — the distrust I detected in those most dear to me as to the motives and intentions which sustained and urged me onward in the evidently unequal struggle. Even at that time the adverse opinion of the majority was a matter of little moment to me ; but to see myself suspected of ambition, or any other than noble motives, by the one or two beings upon whom I had concentrated my whole power of attachment, prostrated my soul in deep despair. And these things were revealed to me at the very time when, assailed as I was on every side, I felt most intensely the need of comforting and re-tempering my spirit in communion with the fraternal souls I had deemed capable of comprehending even my silence, of divining all that I suffered in deliberately renouncing every earthly joy, and of smiling in suffering with me. Without entering into details, I will merely say that it was precisely in this hour of need that these fraternal souls withdrew from me.

When I felt that I was indeed alone in the world — alone, but for my poor mother, far away and unhappy also for my sake — I drew back in terror at the void before me. Then, in that moral desert, doubt came upon me. Perhaps I was wrong, and the world right ? Perhaps my idea was indeed a dream ? Perhaps I had been led, not by an Idea, but by *my* idea ; by the pride of my *own* conception ; the desire of victory rather than the purpose of the victory ; an intellectual egotism, and the cold calculation of an ambitious spirit, drying up and withering the spontaneous and innocent impulses of my heart, which would have led me to the modest virtues of a limited sphere, and to duties near at hand and easy of fulfilment ?

The day on which my soul was furrowed by these doubts I felt myself not only unutterably and supremely wretched ; I felt myself a criminal — conscious of guilt, yet incapable of expiation. The forms of those shot at Alessandria and Chambery rose up before me like the phantoms of a crime and its unavailing remorse. I could not recall them to life. How many mothers had I caused to weep ! How many more must learn to weep should I persist in the attempt to arouse the youth of Italy to noble action, to awaken in them the yearning for a common country ! And if that country were indeed an illusion ? If Italy, exhausted by two epochs of civilisation, were condemned by Providence henceforth to remain subject to younger and more vigorous nations — without a name or a mission of her own — whence had I derived the right of judging the future, and urging hundreds, thousands of men, to the sacrifice of themselves, and of all that they held most dear ?

I will not dwell upon the effect of these doubts

upon my spirit. I will simply say that I suffered so much as to be driven to the confines of madness. At times I started from my sleep at night, and ran to the window in delirium, believing that I heard the voice of Jacopo Ruffini calling to me. At times I felt myself irresistibly impelled to arise and go trembling into the room next my own, fancying that I should see there some friend whom I really knew to be at that time in prison, or hundreds of miles away. The slightest incident — a word, a tone — moved me to tears. Nature, covered with snow as it then was around Grenchen, appeared to me to wear a funereal shroud, beneath which it invited me to sink. I fancied I traced in the faces of those who surrounded me, looks, sometimes of pity, but more often of reproach. I felt every source of life drying up within me ; the death of my very soul. Had that state of mind lasted but a little longer, I must either have gone mad, or ended it with the selfish death of the suicide. Whilst I was thus struggling and sinking beneath my cross, I heard a friend whose room was a few doors distant from mine, answer a young girl, who, having some suspicion of my unhappy condition, was urging him to break in upon my solitude, by saying : *Leave him alone ; he is in his element, conspiring, and happy*. Ah ! how little can men guess the state of mind of others, unless they regard it — and this is rarely done — by the light of a deep affection.

One morning I awoke to find my mind tranquil and my spirit calmed, as one who has passed through a great danger. The first moment of waking had always been one of great wretchedness with me; it was a return to an existence of little other than suffering, and during those months of which I have spoken, that first moment had been, as it were, a summing up of all the unutterable misery I should have to go through during the day. But on that morning it seemed as if nature smiled a smile of consolation upon me, and the light of day appeared to bless and revive the life in my weary frame. The first thought that passed across my spirit was : *your sufferings are the temptation of egotism, and arise from a misconception of life.*

I set myself to re-examine — now that I was able to do so calmly — both myself and surrounding things. I rebuilt my entire edifice of moral philosophy. In fact, the great question of a true or false conception and definition of life dominated all the secondary questions which had roused that hurricane of doubts and terrors, as the conception and definition of life is — whether recognised or not — the primary basis of all philosophy. The ancient religion of India had defined life as *contemplation* ; and hence the inertia, the immobility, and submerging of self in God, of the Arian families.

Christianity had defined life as *expiation* ; and hence earthly sorrows were regarded as trials to be endured with resignation, even with gladness, and without any duty of struggling against them. Hence the earth was viewed as an abode of suffering, and the emancipation of the soul was to be achieved through indifference and contempt for earthly things.

The materialism of the eighteenth century had gone back two thousand years to repeat the pagan definition of life as a search after happiness ; and hence the spirit of egotism it instilled into the souls of men under various disguises ; hence the hateful spectacle of whole classes rising to do battle in the name of the happiness of all men, only to withdraw from the struggle and abandon their allies as soon as they had achieved their own ; hence the instability and inconstancy of the most generous impulses, the sudden desertions whenever suffering overbalanced hope, and the sudden discouragement caused by the first adversity ; hence the setting up of material interests above principles, and the many other evil results of that false theory which still endure.

I perceived that although every instinct of my soul rebelled against that fatal and ignoble definition of life, yet I had not completely freed myself from the dominating influence exercised by it upon the age, and tacitly nourished in me by my early French studies, and the admiration I felt for those who had preached that doctrine ; as well as an instinctive feeling of opposition to those governments and castes who denied the right to happiness of the multitude, in order to keep them prostrate and enslaved. I had combated the evil in others, but not sufficiently in myself. In my own case, and as if the better to seduce me, that false definition of life had thrown off every baser stamp of material desires, and had centred itself in the affections as in an inviolable sanctuary. I ought to have regarded them as a blessing of God, to be accepted with gratitude whensoever it descended to irradiate or cheer my existence ; not demanded them either as a right or as a reward. I had unconsciously made of them the condition of fulfilment of my duties. I had been unable to realise the true ideal of love — love without earthly hope — and had unknowingly worshipped, not love itself, but the joys of love. When these vanished, I had despaired of all things ; as if the joys and sorrows I encountered on the path of life could alter the *aim* I had aspired to reach ; as if the darkness or serenity of Heaven could change the purpose or necessity of the journey.

I had been false to that faith in the immortality of life, and in a progressive series of existences, which, in the eyes of the believer, transforms our sufferings here into the trials and difficulties of one who ascends a steep mountain at the summit of which is God ; a series of existences which are linked together and gradually develop all that on earth is but a germ or promise. I had denied the sun himself because I found myself, in this brief earthly stage, unable to illumine my feeble lamp by his ray. I had been a coward without knowing it. I too had given way to egotism, while I believed myself most free from it, simply because I had transported the *Ego* into a higher and purer sphere than that in which it is adored by the majority.

Life is a mission. Every other definition of life is false, and leads all who accept it astray. Religion, science, philosophy, though still at variance upon many points, all agree in this, that every existence is an *aim*. Were it not so, of what avail were the movement, the Progress, which all are beginning to recognise as the Law of life?

And that aim is *one*: to develop and bring into action all the faculties which constitute and lie dormant in human nature — *Humanity*, — and cause them harmoniously to combine towards the discovery and application of that law. But individuals — according to the time and space in which they live — have various secondary aims, all under the direction of and governed by that one supreme and permanent aim; and all tending to the constant further development and association of the collective faculties and forces. For one man, this secondary aim may be to aid in the moral and intellectual improvement of the few immediately around him; for another, gifted with superior faculties, or placed in more favourable circumstances, the secondary aim is to promote the formation of a Nationality ; to reform the social condition of a people ; to solve a political or religious question.

Our own Dante understood this, when, more than five centuries ago, he spoke of the *great Sea of Being* upon which all existences were led by power divine towards *different ports*.

Mankind is young yet, both in knowledge and power, and a tremendous uncertainty still hangs over the determination of the special aims to which we are bound to devote ourselves. But the logical certainty of their existence is sufficient, and it is enough to know that it is the part of each — if our lives are to be life indeed, and not mere vegetation — to endeavour during the few years granted us on earth, more or less to purify and transform the element, the *medium* in which we live, in harmony with the one transcending aim.

Life is a mission : duty, therefore, its highest law. In the comprehension of that mission, and fulfilment of that duty, lie our means of future progress, the secret of the stage of existence into which we shall be initiated at the conclusion of this earthly stage.

Life is immortal ; but the method and time of evolution through which it progresses is in our own hands. Each of us is bound to purify his own soul as a temple ; to free it from egotism ; to set before himself — with a religious sense of the importance of the study — the problem of his own life ; to search

out what is the most striking, the most urgent need
of the men by whom he is surrounded; then inter-
rogate his own faculties and capacity, and resolutely
and unceasingly apply them to the satisfaction of
that need.   And that examination is not to be undertaken in a spirit of mere analysis, which is incapable
of revealing life, and is ever impotent save when as-
sisting or subserving some ruling synthesis; but by
hearkening to the voice of his own heart, concentrating *all* the faculties of his mind to bear upon the
point, — by the intuition, in short, of a loving soul,
fully impressed with the solemnity of life.   Young
brothers, when once you have conceived and determined your mission within your soul, let naught arrest your steps.   Fulfil it with all your strength;
fulfil it, whether blessed by love or visited by hate;
whether strengthened by association with others, or
in the sad solitude that almost always surrounds the
martyrs of thought.   The path is clear before you;
you are cowards, unfaithful to your own future, if,
in spite of sorrows and delusions, you do not pursue
it to the end.

> *Fortem posce animum, mortis terrore carentem,*
> *Qui spatium vitæ extremum inter munera ponat*
> *Naturæ, qui ferre queat quoscumque labores*
> *Nesciat irasci, cupiat nihil. . .*

These verses of Juvenal sum up all that we should
ask of God, all that once made Rome both mistress
and benefactress of the world.   There is more of the

true philosophy of life in those four lines of one of
our ancient authors, than in fifty volumes of those
sophists who for more than half a century have led
the too plastic mind of youth astray, beneath the dis-
guise of analytic formulæ and learned nomenclature.

I remember a passage of Krasinski, a Polish poet of
great power, unknown in Italy, wherein the Deity
addresses the poet, saying : "Go, and believe in my
name. Think not of thine own glory, but of the
good of those whom I confide to thee. Be calm
amidst the pride, oppression, and scorn of the unjust. These things will pass away, but neither my
thought nor thou wilt pass away. . . Go, and let
action be thy life. Even should thy heart wither in
thy bosom, shouldst thou learn to distrust thy brother
men, and to despair of my support, live in action —
ceaseless, unresting action — and thou wilt survive
all those nourished in vanity, all the happy and il-
lustrious ; thou wilt live again, not in barren illu-
sions, but in the work of ages, and thou wilt become
one of the children of heaven."

The poetry is beautiful and true as any I know.
Yet nevertheless — perhaps because the author, a
Catholic, was unable to extricate himself from the
influence of the doctrines taught by Catholicism of
the purpose of life — there breathes throughout the
lines an ill-repressed spirit of individualism, a promise of reward, that I could wish to see banished from
all souls consecrated to good. The reward assigned

by God will be given ; but we ought not to think of
that. The religion of the future will bid the believer : *Save the souls of others, and leave the care of
thine own to God.* The faith which should guide
us shines forth, I think, more purely in these few
words of another Polish poet, even less known than
Krasinski — Skarga — which I have often repeated
to myself : "The threatening steel flashes before our
eyes, and wretchedness awaits us on the path ; yet
the Lord hath said : *'Onwards, onwards without
rest.'* But whither go we, O Lord ? *'Go on and
die, ye who are bound to die ; go on and suffer, ye
who are bound to suffer.'* "

How I was at length enabled to proffer these
words ; through what process of intellectual labour
I succeeded in arriving at a confirmation of my first
faith, and resolved to work on so long as life should
last, whatever the sorrows and revilings that might
assail me, towards the great aim which had been revealed to me in the prison of Savona — the republican unity of my country — I cannot detail here ; nor
would it avail. I noted down at that time a record
of the trials and struggles I underwent, and the reflections which redeemed me, in long fragments of a
work fashioned after the model of Ortis, which I intended to publish anonymously, under the title of
Records of an Unknown. I carried them with me,
written in minute characters upon very thin paper,
to Rome, and lost them in passing through France on

my return.   Were I now to endeavour to re-write the feelings and impressions of that period, I should find it impossible.

I came to my better self alone, without aid from others, through the help of a religious conception which I verified by history.   From the idea of God I descended to the conception of progress ; from the conception of progress to a true conception of life ; to faith in a mission and its logical consequence — duty the supreme rule of life ; and having reached that faith, I swore to myself that nothing in this world should again make me doubt or forsake it.   It was, as Dante says, passing through martyrdom to peace * — a *"forced and despairing peace"* I do not deny — for I fraternised with sorrow, and enwrapped myself in it as in a mantle ; but yet it was peace, for I learned to suffer without rebellion, and to live calmly, and in harmony with my own spirit.   I bade a long sad farewell to all individual hopes for me on earth.   I dug with my own hands the grave, not of my affections, — God is my witness that now, greyheaded, I feel them yet as in the days of my earliest youth, — but to all the desires, exigencies, and ineffable comforts of affection ; and I covered the earth over that grave, so that none might ever know the *Ego* buried beneath.   From reasons —

---

* "Da martirio
E da esiglio venne a questa pace."
                                        Paradiso.

some of them apparent, some of them unknown —
my life was, is, and, were it not near the end, would
remain unhappy ; but never since that time have I for
an instant allowed myself to think that my own un-
happiness could in any way influence my actions.
I reverently bless God the Father for what consolations of affection — I can conceive of no other — He
has vouchsafed to me in my later years ; and in them
I gather strength to struggle with the occasional re-
turns of weariness of existence. But even were these
consolations denied me, I believe I should still be
what I am. Whether the sun shine with the serene
splendour of an Italian morn, or the leaden corpse-
like hue of the northern mist be above us, I cannot
see that it changes our duty. God dwells above the
earthly heaven, and the holy stars of faith and the
future still shine within our own souls, even though
their light consume itself unreflected as the sepul-
chral lamp.

XI

ON THE FAILURE OF THE REVOLUTIONS OF 1848

Europe was shaken to her foundations. A score
of revolutions broke out in as many different re-
gions. France repudiated the last formula of absolutism — the "middle-class monarchy." Germany,
calm, thoughtful Germany, found a dozen centres of
insurrection erupting on her soil. Vienna heard the

lion's roar of her populace, and the Emperor fled.
The Pope fled from Rome.   The lava of revolution
boiled over from Milan to Pest, from Venice to Ber-
lin, from Rome to Posen.   "Liberty, Independence,
Right ! "   Such the motto on flags that just now
were waving over two thirds of Europe.   And then
— failure everywhere !   The blood of our brave, the
tears of our mothers, bathe naught but crosses on the
graves of our martyrs.   Victory deserted our camp,
and today our cry has perforce to be the cry we
raised fifteen years ago.   Once more we have to
sound the clarions of 1835 !

Now there must be some deep reason for our
failure, something inherent in the organisation of
our Party.   We surpass our adversaries in courage,
in devotion, in our sense of the needs of the masses.
Wherever, in these last insurrections, we faced the
enemy on equal terms, one to one, people against
government, the victory was ours.   And we did not
abuse our victory.   Wherever we attained power
we discharged the hangman.   Our hands are pure.
Along with our poverty and our faith we carry clean
consciences with us into exile.

Why then is Reaction triumphant ?

Yes — you have said it !   The reason lies in ourselves, in our lack of organisation, in the dismemberment of our rank and file that has resulted from
conflicting systems of thought, systems now absurd,
now dangerous, always imperfect and immature, but

always defended in a fierce and bigoted spirit of intolerance. It lies in our mistrust of each other, in our perpetual and altogether wretched vanities, in our absolute lack of that capacity for orderly discipline which alone produces great things ; in the scattering of our forces through multitudes of small centres and numberless small sects that are all-powerful for disorganisation, but impotent for concerted action. The reason lies in a worship of material interests that has gradually made its way into our schools at the expense of the holy ideals, at the expense of our effort for education which alone can legitimise our struggle, at the expense of our feeling for Life and Life's mission. The reason lies in our having forgotten God, forgotten His law of love, forgotten self-sacrifice and moral progress, the solemn religious tradition of humanity — all things that we have replaced with the concept of "welfare," with Volney's catechism, with Bentham's principle of self-interest, with indifference to truths of an order higher than the earthly which are alone capable of transforming the world. The reason lies in a crude spirit of nationalism that has supplanted the spirit of nationality, in a foolish conviction on the part of each people that it is capable of solving all its social, political and economic problems with its own resources and to its own best advantage. The reason lies in our forgetfulness of the great truths that the cause of the peoples is one cause ; that country must rest upon humanity; that when revolutions cease to profess a cult of self-sacrifice for all who suffer and fight, they wear themselves out in movements in a circle and fail; that the objective in all our wars, and the only force that is able to vanquish an alliance of Powers which has issued from privilege and selfishness must be the Holy Alliance of the Nations. Lamartine's manifesto killed the French Republic, just as the language of narrow-minded nationalism that was used at Frankfurt killed the revolution in Germany, and just as the fatal idea of aggrandisement for the House of Savoy killed the revolution in Italy.

Today more than ever we must combat these deadly tendencies. The evil is within us. We must overcome it or perish. The truth must be frankly proclaimed even though it indicts us. Those who are leading us astray may be angry at the revelation, but the good sense of the masses may profit by it. As for our enemies, their destinies depend upon the direction we give to our work. Their power lives only because of our mistakes. We are advancing in stormy weather, but just ahead shines the sun of God, radiant, eternal. For a time our enemies may veil it from our eyes so that we cannot see it. Never, never can they erase it from the sky. By the grace of God Europe has been liberated by the days of Marathon through which we have just passed. On those days the principle of inertia was vanquished

for ever, Freedom gave its baptism to our soil, and
Europe started on the way. She is still on the way,
and no wretched scrolls of diplomatic or princely
parchment will again be able to halt her.

XII

DOCTRINAIRES OF 1830

For many years a sect of men had existed in
France, who, as far as action, conspiracy, or danger
were concerned, had ever held aloof from the camp
of combatants, but who were united with them in
the desire of overthrowing the retrograde supporters
of *Right Divine*. These men were baptized by the
people — I believe from their lack of any real doctrine — by the name of the *Doctrinaires*. They
called themselves by the absurd and hypocritical
name of *Moderates* — a name adopted now by our
Italian copyists of every evil thing in France ; as if
there could exist *moderation* in the choice between
good and evil, the truth and falsehood, advance and
retrogression.

The history of the sect may be traced back as far
as the first Committee of the Constitution, formed
in the National Assembly during the great Revolution. Their programme — more or less openly
avowed — was a monarchy, tempered by the intervention of two legislative chambers, to be composed

of the nobility and wealthy bourgeoisie ; the people being excluded.

The power and influence of the nobility having been weakened by the natural course of things, the principal element of this sect was the bourgeoisie ; and their leaders at that day were Broglie, Royer Collard, Guizot, Cousin, Thiers, Rossi, Odillon Barrot, Dupin, Sebastiani, Casimir Perier, etc.

Lafayette, a man weak by nature, was a republican in belief, although a monarchist in all the acts of his life. The friendship of Washington, an honesty above suspicion, and a series of peculiar circumstances, had given him a reputation greater than his deserts. He handed over the people's victory to this sect in 1830, thus affording new proof of the fact, that every revolution that identifies its own destiny with that of an individual — be he who or what he may — unconsciously prepares the way for its own ruin.

The vagueness and generality of their own formulæ, their adoption of many phrases borrowed from our party, as well as their personal friendship with many of the boldest of its members, afforded, or appeared to afford, good grounds for hoping that neither vanity nor lust of power would induce them to betray the cause. And their unceasing legal opposition did in fact prepare the way for the desired revolution, by forcing the monarchy to extreme measures of repression. The more advanced party

decided to admit these men into their ranks, in order
to increase their own importance ; and they preached
them up as men who were prepared, if once in power,
to satisfy all the aspirations and demands of the party
of the future, provided their strength and universal-
ity should have been proved by the fact of action.

But by admitting them into their ranks, the advanced party accepted at the same time their tendency to compromise, their Jesuitical reservation and
reticence, their fatal tactics of *opportunity*, and their
hypocritical cry of *Vive la Charte* — a cry well
adapted to be used as a weapon in their legal battles
in the Chamber of Deputies, but calculated to lead
the people astray from the true aim, when substituted
to their own honest cry of *Vive la Revolution*.

And when the moment of revolution came, that
hypocritical cry, and the weakness of Lafayette com-
bined, did in fact open the way for the Moderates,
and enable them to take the direction of it into their
own hands, and dwindle its results to a mere revision
of the Charter, and substitution of the younger for
the elder branch of the Bourbons.

The same spirit of *legality* which had presided
over the hypocritical parliamentary struggle for fifteen years, induced Lafayette to entrust the destinies
of the revolution to the keeping of the 221 members
of the opposition, who, in their turn, yielded them
up to Louis Philippe. Thus, in spite of the tardy
protests of those who had fought the battles of the

revolution, they improvised what they called by the absurd and lying name of the republican monarchy ; as if the words Monarchy and Republic did not represent two forms of government essentially and radically opposed.

Events are under the inexorable dominion of logic. Every violation of faith in principles carries along with it certain and inevitable consequences of strife and suffering which none may prevent. When this inevitable moment of struggle arrived, the *Moderates* — that is to say, the representatives of the *bourgeoisie* — deliberately separated themselves from the people whose aid they had implored while it was essential to their own triumph. Their defection was shamelessly open, and forms one of the ugliest pages of the history of France ; for two thirds of the intellect of the country are implicated in its disgrace. All those who remained faithful to the republican ideal were treated as destructive demagogues ; the working men as a dangerous element only to be held in check by the necessity of mechanical labour and a state of dependence upon the capitalists, and to be excluded from all public life by being deprived of all political rights. A little later, a member of the ministry compared them to the *barbarians* who invaded Rome.

I well remember the mute astonishment and grief with which, still young in years and feelings, we witnessed that spectacle of moral dissolution. But a few years before we had regarded these very men as the standard-bearers of the party whose aim was the re-generation of Europe. From their writings, their speeches, and their eloquent lectures, delivered to the youth of France in 1828–29, and read by us with affection and admiration, we had drawn alike inspiration and the courage to dare. We had transcribed their pages, and passed them from one to another, swearing fidelity to the principles they contained.

And now every day brought us fresh news of some solemn betrayal of those sacred principles uttered by the same lips ; every day our hearts were wounded by a fresh delusion ; every day we saw yet another of those idols to whom we had burned our heart's incense, fall from his pedestal.

It was Cousin, the restorer of philosophical discipline, the fervid apostle of a progress knowing no limits save those of time itself, who, speaking of the revolution, declared, that *three days had in no way changed the face of things.*

It was Guizot who said, *the best form of government was that least liked by the people.*

And a third — one who had twenty times accused the government of Charles X of servile egotism — endeavoured to justify their abandonment of the cause of the peoples by solemnly uttering the impious words — *The blood of France should be shed for France alone.*

Another announced the downfall of heroic Poland, by saying, *Order reigns in Warsaw.*

Some of these men declared that the formula of *each for himself* was the basis of all political doctrine ; others cut short all hope of any amelioration of the condition of the poorer classes, by inaugurating their economical science with another formula — a translation of the political one just quoted — that of *laissez faire*. Others again separated the *principle* from the *fact*, the spirit from its *material manifestation*, and disinherited society of all belief by declaring that *the law is atheist !* Thiers denied Armand Carrel, and all those with whom he had fought the battles of liberty in the *National* ; Barthelemy sold the pen with which he had written the *Nemesis* to the minister who paid his debts.

Ah ! who can say what germs of egotism were sown in the hearts of the young generation by these evil examples !

The image of many a youth, then good, and devoted to the cause of truth, passes before me now like a pale phantom of the first years of my political life. Weak, and accustomed to seek inspiration from the outward and external, rather than to derive it from within, I saw them assailed by delusion and discouragement at that time, — I saw them waver in their faith, slacken in affection, and enter unconsciously upon the path that leads to inert misanthropy on the one hand, and, on the other, to that hideous form of egotism which drapes itself in I know not what experimental semi-science, which they term *practical*.

We held on, because ours was a religious faith, and not the mere reaction of rights denied, or desire of prevailing in our turn over the rulers of the day ; we held on, but the light of that trust and confidence that strengthens the soul to labour was quenched for ever within us. It is true that we then said to one another, with Italian pride, *Our countrymen will be better than these men are*. But even from that illusion I was doomed to stand, with sorrow — corrected.

Were they in fact traitors ? Did these deserters from our banner yield to the suggestions of vulgar egotism, and the lust of power, which they hoped to acquire more rapidly and completely as adherents of the monarchy ? Some of them were no doubt corrupt and despicable even to that point. But the majority simply yielded to the logical consequences of a false doctrine — a doctrine which we Italians have not as yet studied with sufficient gravity and attention.

Their philosophy was not the philosophy of the future. Self was its starting-point, and self the goal. Teaching as it did the sovereignty of the *individual*, it was impossible it should rise to the idea of a supreme duty governing all the acts of life.

In politics they had not gone beyond the theory of

rights — a theory which, destitute of all deep faith in *collective* man, necessarily led to their formula of "each for himself."

Their whole history and tradition dated from this doctrine, which — when carefully sifted and examined — results in the justification of the stronger individuality, and, consequently, of the powers that be.

Such were they all — flatterers of power one day and of the people the next ; but always worshippers of any powerful fact, or of anything that appeared likely to become such.

In order to perceive this worship of the *fact* in these men, it is enough to read with attention Thiers's *History of the Revolution* — by which, however, he acquired so great reputation among the youth of that day — and observe how he admires in that revolution, not the victory of eternal right, but the grandeur of a gigantic fact, and bows down with equal reverence before the audacity of the *Montagne* of the *eighteenth Fructidor* and the *eighteenth Brumaire.*

It is enough to observe how — forgetting that the corruption of the Republic began with the Directory ; forgetting the monarchical tendencies of the Club of Clichy ; forgetting the germs of military and bourgeoisie aristocracy already apparent, and the idea of the power of one nation then substituted to the idea of emancipation of all ; but struck with the strength of France abroad — he exalts

the period *when France was mistress of the whole
extent of territory between the Rhine and the Pyre-
nees, from the Alps to the sea; when the arms of
Spain and Holland were united with hers, and half
Europe was at the feet of the Directory.* And again,
when speaking of the changes introduced into the
cisalpine constitution through the instrumentality of
a simple *envoyé* from Paris, Trouvé, he rashly adds:
*But the manner was of little moment; it would have
been absurd if France, the creatrix of those Republics, had not exerted her authority to govern them
according to her own will and pleasure.*

And in order to judge how little the people had
to expect from that school, it is enough to remember
the lines written in the *Journal des Débats*, the organ
of the *Doctrinaires*, while the struggle was at its
height. *Strengthen the salutary dominion of the
bourgeoisie, ever the friend of order and repose; for
who are in fact the sufferers from the law of primo-
geniture? the bourgeoisie, who have property to
divide among their children, and not the people, who
possess nothing. Who are injured by the three per
cent? the bourgeoisie. Who by the censorship?
the bourgeoisie, who desire to read and to think
freely, and not the people, who have no time to think
of anything but maintaining their existence by in-
cessant labour.*

But the youth of that day were rash and thought-
less. Enamoured of certain periods in those multi-

ple lives, and fascinated by the idea of concentrating
the greatest possible number of intellectual elements
around the cause of liberty, they forgot that no good
or useful revolution is possible without morality ;
and that the union of heterogeneous elements, though
possible after a victory, is certain to be fatal if attempted before the victory is achieved.

They too, in virtue of their doctrine, were worshippers of fact.   Thiers had said, that *in forming
a judgment upon public matters, everything depends
upon the point of view taken, and the position of
the person judging.*   Guizot had written that *it is
an error to take up one's position outside the victorious camp ; any power that does so is false to itself, and betrays its own nature.   It is madness to
separate one's self from the side of power, when that
power assumes the character of a necessity.*

Why did the youth of France forget those words ?
The *victorious camp* in 1830 was the camp of the
bourgeoisie.   How then could they hope that the
Moderates would join the camp of the people ?
How could they expect them to deduce consequences adverse to the tendency of their own doctrines, and rush into the ranks of duty and martyrdom, to realise an aim vaster than their own ; when
by stopping short they attained liberty, power, and
wealth for themselves, added to the satisfaction of
their pride in the logical results of their own narrow

doctrine ? We betrayed ourselves even more than we were betrayed by them.

Every political system, when carefully analysed, will be found to be derived from a system of philosophy. Ideas precede and generate facts. The necessity of harmonising theory and practice is as much a law in politics as in any other thing. No system of practice can be effectually destroyed, without overcoming or converting the belief upon which it is based.

Every true revolution is a programme ; and derived from a new, general, positive, and organic principle. The first thing necessary is to accept that principle. Its development must then be confided to men who are believers in it, and emancipated from every tie or connection with any principle of an opposite nature.

Generally speaking, the reverse of this is done. The people entrust the destinies of their revolutions to men influential either by position or name, who have always represented opposite aims, and have merely joined the ranks of the combatants from reaction against a power by which they were oppressed or despised.

Hence follow the inevitable consequences of delusion — violent irritation and new warfare between the conflicting elements, anarchy, and civil war.

The irritation of the French people against the

men whom, through a political error, they had accepted as leaders, and who naturally betrayed their hopes, created the germs of an unjust and impotent *sectarian socialism*, which, from the terror inspired by its doctrines in the majority of the nation, resulted at a later period in the deplorable experiment of the empire. Similar errors threaten our rising Italy with similar consequences ; and it is for this reason that I speak at some length of this period of French history, which I believe to have been hitherto misunderstood.

The authors of the revolution of 1830, by starting from a false calculation of opportunity, and denying in practice the potent initiative of a principle they professed in theory ; by accepting from men of a different belief a method of warfare which, instead of driving the enemy upon new and unknown ground, sought to defeat them upon their own ; by invoking, as a mere matter of strategy, a Charter in which they did not believe, and a monarchical Pact they were resolved to overthrow — followed the example of the *opposition* in those Jesuitical and immoral artifices which they had themselves designated as the *fifteen years' farce*.

By so doing — although without intending it — they substituted a war of names for a war of things ; led the national mind in a false direction, destroyed all sense of dignity in individuals, and of right in the masses ; and restrained the spirit of the revolution within the narrow compass of a document altogether unequal to the necessities of the times. They introduced disloyalty into the holy battle of progress, and prepared the way for the system of corruption realised by Louis Philippe.

The *Revolutionist* — as I understand the word — has a creed, a faith ; the *Reactionist* has none. He has instincts, passions, often generous in their origin, but easily deviated or corrupted by disappointments, or the seductions of power, so soon as years have cooled his enthusiasm and his youthful blood. The Revolutionist is he to whom observation has shown the existence of a grave social grievance or immorality — to whom intelligence has shown a remedy — and to whom the voice of conscience, enlightened by a religious conception of the human mission here below, has revealed the inexorable duty of devoting himself to the application of the remedy, and extirpation of the evil.

The *reactionist* is one urged by a sentiment of rebellion against injustice — innate in minds gifted with any power — and very often by the pain and irritation consequent on being unable to assume his true place in the social order ; to seek to better his own condition, with the help of all who suffer under similar distress.

The revolutionist will pursue his forward march, whatever his individual position, so long as the evil endures ; the reactionist will probably stop short as soon as the injustice shall cease with regard to himself, or as soon as the overthrow of the power attacked shall have satisfied his self-love, and mitigated the sense of rebellion within him.

The revolutionist may be mistaken as to the remedy to be applied : he may anticipate too much from the immediate future, and substitute his individual intuition to the common sense of the masses ; but he will produce no grave disorder in society. If his conception be premature, and meet with no echo, he will perish in the struggle almost alone ; while the reactionist, careful to excite all the war-like and active passions of the multitude and of the young, and to leave the solution of the problem uncertain, so as to allow each man the hope of seeing his own adopted, will always meet with a powerful response to his appeal.

The aim of the one is always to *found* ; that of the other is to *destroy*. The first is a man of progress ; the second of opposition. The first argues from, and seeks to enthrone, a *law* ; the second from a *fact*, and ends in the consecration of force.

With the first, it is a question of principle : he states his purpose frankly, proceeds in a straight line, neglects what are called tactics, renounces many elements of success, trusting in the power of truth ; commits a thousand petty errors, but redeems them all by the enunciation of certain general maxims, sooner or later of use.

With the reactionist details are everything : he understands to perfection that analysis which decomposes and dissolves ; in his hands every question becomes a question of men, and every war a skirmish. His eloquence is lively, supple, and occasionally brilliant ; while the revolutionist, often monotonous and dry, is always logical. He may fail to achieve his aim, but if he reach it once, it is for ever ; while the victories of the reactionist, though sometimes splendid, are never durable. The first invokes duty, the second right. A strong religious leaning influences the acts of the first, even when, through an intellectual contradiction, he professes the reverse : the second is irreligious and materialist even when he proffers the name of God ; with him the present always tops the future, and material interest takes precedence of moral progress.

The men of the first class, accustomed to willing sacrifice, labour less for the generation that lives around them, than for the generations to come ; the triumph of the ideas they cast upon the world is slow, but infallible and decisive : the men of the second class often win victories for their contemporaries, but their children will enjoy none of the fruits.

The first are the prophets of humanity, the second are the mere agitators of mankind ; and bitter repentance ever awaits the people that commits its destinies into their hands.

MAZZINI

GIUSSEPPE MAZZINI was born at Genoa, June 22, 1805, into
home of markedly religious influence, his parents being Ja
senists. After graduating in law at the University of Geno
Mazzini became a member of the secret society of the Ca
bonari. Three years later, however, he was denounced to th
police and imprisoned at Savona for six months. During th
imprisonment, he had the first clear view of his mission as
politico-religious prophet. On his release, he became an exil
living in France, Switzerland and, finally, London. In 183
Mazzini founded "Young Italy." He was an active conspirato
all his life, fomenting armed insurrections against the King
dom of Piedmont, the Austrian Empire, the Papal States, an
the Kingdom of Naples. In 1857, he was condemned to deat
in absentia by Cavour's Piedmontese government for a ne
attempt at insurrection. After the achievement of Italian unit
he re-entered Italy illegally in 1872 and died at Pisa on Marc
10th of that same year.